POLITICAL ECONOMY IN NINETEENTH-CENTURY AMERICA

Selected and Introduced by
Morgen Witzel

Volume 5

History of American Thought

Political Economy in Nineteenth-Century America

Selected and Introduced by **Morgen Witzel**

Volume 1
Mathew Carey
Essays on Political Economy, 1822

Volume 2
Francis Wayland
The Elements of Political Economy, 1837

Volume 3
George Tucker
Political Economy for the People, 1859

Volume 4
Amasa Walker
The Science of Wealth: A Manual of Political Economy, 1866

Volume 5
William Graham Sumner
Problems in Political Economy, 1884 and
Essays on Political Economy, 1885

Volume 6
Francis A. Walker
Political Economy, 1892

Printed in England by Antony Rowe Ltd, Chippenham

PROBLEMS IN POLITICAL ECONOMY

ESSAYS ON POLITICAL ECONOMY

William Graham Sumner

THOEMMES PRESS

Published by Thoemmes Press, 2003

Thoemmes Press
11 Great George Street
Bristol BS1 5RR, England

http://www.thoemmes.com

Political Economy in Nineteenth-Century America
6 Volumes : ISBN 1 84371 048 X

British Library Cataloguing-in-Publication Data
A CIP record of this title is available from the British Library

This book is printed on acid-free paper, sewn, and
cased in a durable buckram.

PROBLEMS

IN

POLITICAL ECONOMY

BY

WILLIAM GRAHAM SUMNER

PROFESSOR OF POLITICAL AND SOCIAL SCIENCE IN YALE COLLEGE

NEW YORK

HENRY HOLT AND COMPANY

1884

CONTENTS.

PREFACE.

When I began to make this collection of problems I intended to make only a small pamphlet for use in my own class-room. The enterprise has grown, however, until it has seemed better to make a book and publish it. Hence a few words of explanation are here needed.

I have long used problems and fallacies as auxiliary to my other class-room work. The object of such exercises is to break up the routine of text-book recitations, to encourage wider study of scientific treatises, and to develop some independent power of thinking, and of applying the principles which have been learned. In the present state of political economy it seems especially desirable to study subjects, and not text-books. These problems are intended to bring forward the subjects or topics which should be studied, and to guide the student to an investigation of them with the aid of the teacher, and by the use of the leading treatises in the science. The problems are, in their form, almost all "leading," and effort has been made to put them in such a way that a student who has already studied an elementary text-book can deal with them. When possible, they have been put in that form in which they present themselves in practice. My aim has been to limit the references as much as possible in number, and to concentrate them on the following books: Rogers's Adam Smith, Mill's Principles, Jevons' Theory, Marshall's Economics of Industry, Cairnes's Principles, Walker's Political Economy, and Cossa's Guide. A "Loan Library of Political Economy" has been formed as a part of the scheme, from which each student can obtain a copy of each of the above books for use so long as he desires. I have found, however, that, if the problems were to have any range and variety, I must enlarge the range of the references far beyond my original intention. I give below a list of all the books to which reference is made under the problems. The library will contain these in numbers proportioned to their usefulness.

While I was at work on these problems Milnes' collection of 2,000 questions and problems from English examination papers was published. I have to acknowledge my obligations to that collection. I have borrowed some problems from it; others I have adapted. They are marked by an M. with the number in Milnes' collection, thus: (M. 100). Many have been suggested to me by reading that collection. I have given credit whenever the suggestion was so close that I could specify the question in Milnes' collection which suggested mine. This was not always possible, and so the present general acknowledgment must cover the rest.

The problems here given are of very unequal difficulty and importance. A primary classification is made by printing the numbers of those which I should reserve for examination at a later stage of study with thin faced numerals.

I am indebted to Prof. H. W. Farnam and Mr. Arthur Hadley for valuable aid and suggestions.

W. G. S.

YALE COLLEGE, December, 1883.

FULL TITLES OF BOOKS CITED.

Accounts and Papers, Session [Parliament] 1868-9, vol. 35, (Public Finances since 1688).

Baden-Powell, State Aid and State Interference. Chapman & Hall, 1882.

Bagehot, Lombard Street. Scribner, Armstrong & Co., 1873.

Banker's Magazine. New York.

Brodrick, English Land and English Landlords. Cassel & Co., 1881.

Cairnes, Logical Method of Political Economy. Macmillan, 1875.

Cairnes, Some Principles of Political Economy. Harpers.

Cairnes, Essays in Political Economy, Theoretical and Applied. Macmillan, 1873.

Chevalier, *Économie Politique*. Paris, 1866.

Chevalier, On Gold (Translated). Appleton, 1859.

Cossa, Guide to the Study of Political Economy (Translated). Macmillan, 1880.

Crump, English Manual of Banking. Longmans, 1877.

Cunningham, Growth of English Industry and Commerce. Cambridge, University Press, 1882.

DeBroglie, *Le Libre Échange et L'Impot*. Paris, 1879.

DeLavelaye, Primitive Property (Translated). Macmillan, 1878.

Dictionnaire de l'Économie Politique. Guillaumin, 1854.

Fawcett, Political Economy, 6th Ed. Macmillan, 1883.

Fawcett, Pauperism. Macmillan, 1871.

Fawcett, Free Trade and Protection. Macmillan, 1878.

Ford, American Citizen's Manual. Putnam, 1883.

Giffen, Essays in Finance. Geo. Bell & Sons, 1880.

Gilbart, The Principles and Practice of Banking. Bell & Daldy, 1871.

Goschen, Theory of the Foreign Exchanges. E. Wilson, 1875.
Grant, Recess Studies. Edmonston & Douglas, Edinburgh, 1870.
Hankey, The Principles of Banking. Effingham Wilson, 1873.
Hertzka, *Währung und Handel.* Wien, 1876.
Holyoake, History of Coöperation in England. Lippincott, 1875.
Horton, Silver and Gold. R. Clarke & Co., 1876.
Humboldt, Sphere and Duties of Government. London, 1854.
Hamilton. National Debt of Great Britain. Carey, 1816.
Jevons, Theory of Political Economy. Macmillan, 1871.
Jevons, Money and the Mechanism of Exchange. Appleton, 1875.
Jevons, The Coal Question. Macmillan, 1866.
Jevons, Methods of Social Reform. Macmillan, 1883.
Lalor, Cyclopedia of Political Science, etc. Rand, McNally & Co., 1882.
Leroy-Beaulieu, *Science des Finances.* Guillaumin, 1877.
Letourneau, Sociology (Translated). Chapman & Hall, 1881.
Levi, History of British Commerce. Murray, 1880.
Macleod, Principles of Economical Philosophy. Longmans, 1872.
Macleod, Dictionary of Political Economy. Longmans, 1863.
Maine, Village Communities. Murray, 1871.
Mann, Paper Money. Appleton, 1872.
Marshall, Economics of Industry. Macmillan, 1879.
Martineau, History of England. Boston, 1865.
McCulloch's Adam Smith. Longmans, 1838.
Mill, Political Economy. Longmans, 1878.
Mill, Logic. Harpers, 1870.
Mill, Liberty. Longmans, 1865.
Milnes, Problems in Political Economy. Sonnenschein, 1882.
Molesworth, History of England. Chapman & Hall, 1874.
Mongredien, History of the Free Trade Movement in England. Cassell & Co.
Mongredien, Wealth Creation. Cassell & Co., 1882.
Price, Practical Political Economy. Kegan Paul & Co., 1878.
Princeton Review, November, 1879, Bimetalism.
Princeton Review, March, 1881, The Argument Against Protective Taxes.
Princeton Review, November, 1881, Sociology.

Princeton Review, November, 1882, Wages.

Probyn, Systems of Land Tenure in Various Countries. Cassell & Co.

Ricardo, Works, Edited by McCulloch. Murray, 1881.

Richardson, H. A., National Banks. Harpers.

Richardson, W. A., Public Debt and National Banking Laws of the United States. Washington, 1873.

Rogers, History of Agriculture and Prices in England. Clarendon Press, 1866.

Roscher, Political Economy (translated). Callaghan, 1878.

Say, *Rapport sur le Payement de l'Indemnité de Guerre*, in his Translation of Goschen, *Theorie des Changes*. Guillaumin, 1875.

Seebohm, The English Village Community. Longmans, 1883.

Seybert, Statistical Annals. Philadelphia, 1818.

Seyd on Bullion and Foreign Exchanges. Effingham Wilson, 1868.

Sidgwick, Principles of Political Economy. Macmillan, 1883.

Smith, Adam, Wealth of Nations, edited by Rogers. Clarendon Press, 1880.

Smith, Adam, edited by McCulloch, see McCulloch.

Soetbeer, *Petermann's Mittheilungen*, *Ergänzungsheft*, *Nr. 57*, *Edelmetall-produktion*. Gotha, 1879.

Spencer, Study of Sociology. Appleton, 1874.

Spencer, Principles of Sociology. Appleton, 1883.

Spencer, Biology. Appleton. 1874.

Spencer, Social Statics. Appleton, 1863.

Spencer, Essays, Moral, Political and Esthetic. Appleton, 1872.

Sumner, Life of Jackson. Houghton, Mifflin & Co., 1882.

Sumner, Argument before the Tariff Commission, 1882.

Sumner, History of Protection in the United States. Putnam.

Sumner, What Social Classes Owe to Each Other. Harpers, 1883.

Sumner, see "Princeton Review."

Thornton, On Labor. Macmillan, 1870.

Walker, Political Economy. Holt, 1883.

Walker, Money. Holt, 1878.

Walker, Money, Trade and Industry. Holt, 1879.

Walker, Land and its Rent. Little & Brown, 1883.

Wallace, Russia. Holt, 1877.

Walras, *Éléments d' Économie Politique Pure.* Lausanne, 1874.

Ward, Dynamic Sociology. Appleton, 1883.

Wilson, The National Budget. Macmillan, 1882.

Woolsey, Political Science; or, The State. Scribner, Armstrong & Co., 1878.

ECONOMIC PROBLEMS.

I.

GENERAL DEFINITIONS.

1. Discuss the following definitions of political economy: It is the science of value.

It is the science of exchanges.

It is the science which treats of the production, exchange and distribution of wealth.

Political economy, or economics, is the name of that body of knowledge which relates to wealth.

Political economy is the science which investigates the laws of the material welfare of human societies.

Cairnes, Logical Method, 57.

2. Is political economy not a science (1) because, as is alleged, it cannot predict economic phenomena; (2) because, as is alleged, it has not won a body of positive and ascertained results? What is a science? or what is the essential condition that any discipline may become a science?

Marshall, 2.

3. Sociology is the science of life in society. Political economy is that branch of sociology which treats of the industrial organization of society. Expand the notion and definition of sociology and explain what that conception of political economy is which is here presented.

4. Price says that it is silly to call political economy a science; that supply and demand, the law of population, etc., are only familiar facts of intelligent observation. *Per contra*, he affirms that political economy is "the application of common sense to familiar processes. It explains their nature and manner of working. It analyzes and thinks out practices which are universal except when thwarted by artificial theory."—Criticise this view of political economy as antithetical to the notion of a science. What is it to think out a practice? What is a practice which would be universal, if not thwarted? What is an artificial theory? How can a theory thwart a practice?

Price, 10–15.

5. Wealth is any material good which satisfies a desire of man, and which is not gratuitous. It is used as a collective term, for the general conception of such goods, and, when it describes the subject or aim of political economy, it carries with it the notion of abundance.—Criticise and

correct this definition. Do you include in your definition the following? Honesty, health, skill, "the moral, intellectual, and physical natures" of the people, a patent right, a copy-right, a bill of exchange, the voice of a singer, a good harbor, climate, and sunlight. Do you infer, for instance from Price's discussion, that economists need *not* continue the effort to formulate a satisfactory definition of wealth?

Price, 23–30. Marshall, 6. Sidgwick, Chap. III.
Adam Smith, I., 1, Rogers's note.

6. If a census were taken of the wealth of the country ought the owners of land to return it at its market value? Is the land a part of the national wealth? Ought the owners of government bonds to include them in the return? If they did so, and if the returns were added up, the national debt would be counted into the sum of the national wealth. Would that be right? If A sells to B a bale of cotton for $500 and B gives a promissory note for it, ought B to return the cotton and A the note? If A has a certificate of stock in a railroad, ought the railroad officers to return the railroad and ought A to return the stock?

Adam Smith, I., 254, Rogers's note.

7. "Because political economy confines itself to discovering the laws of wealth, it has, by some, been called derisively, the gospel of mammon. In reply to this sneer it would be enough to say that, while wealth is not the sole interest of mankind, perhaps not the highest interest, it is yet of vast concern, of vital concern to individuals and to communities. As such it deserves to be studied. Now, if it is to be studied at all, it will best be studied by itself."—Vindicate in detail this view of political economy and show the relation of political economy to other interests.

Walker, Pol. Ec., 1, 2.

8. If there should be a scarcity of houses in the city of Washington this winter, would that fact constitute a problem requiring the attention of the economists of the country? How does your answer bear on the sphere of political economy and the opinions of the professorial socialists?

9. It has been said that the free play of economic forces would produce, not the best conceivable, but the worst conceivable, state of society. Show the absurdity of this statement.

10. What are economic forces? What are economic laws? Are economic laws subject to exceptions—like laws of grammar? Are economic laws like the ten commandments? Are they like Acts of Congress? Are they like laws

of physics? Can we "violate" them? What is the limit of what we can do with economic forces? If economic laws are described as expressing a "tendency," what is meant? What objection is there to that description of them?

Marshall, 3. Cairnes, Logical Method, 18.
Cairnes, Principles, 184. Mill's Logic, Book III., Chap. 10, §5.
Cossa, 7. Sidgwick, 24. Spencer, Study of Sociology, 22.

11. A writer who ridicules the notion of natural or scientific laws in political economy cites "property" as a proof that no such laws exist. Show the fallacy.

12. Distinguish between the science and art of political economy; between political economy and politics.

Walker, Pol. Econ., 20–22. Cossa, 6, 11–13.

13. Is it a valid distinction to say that the science of political economy investigates what is; the art, what ought to be?

Sidgwick, 23–26, also 402.

14. Does the art of political economy mean, or include, the art of getting rich, or the art of conducting business, or the art of speculation, or the art of investing capital in stocks, bonds, lands, etc., or the art of conducting the finances of a nation, or the art of legislating on trade, industry, and finance? Give reasons for including or excluding each of these things.

15. Is political economy a "moral" science? If so, according to what classification of the sciences is it so classed? and what is meant by so denominating it?

Cairnes, Logical Method, 31, 37.

16. Is political economy a deductive or an inductive science? What difference does it make which it is

Cairnes, Logical Method, 60 fg. Sidgwick, Chap. III.

17. Is imagination a force in political economy? If so, give all the illustrations you can. Discuss delusion, fraud, falsehood, prejudice, habit, tradition, patriotism and affection, so far as you think that an economist ought to take account of them.

Ought there to be any difference in a textbook of political economy for an English college and for a college in India?

Walker, Polit. Econ., 23.

18. If it is said: "Some people struggle to keep up false appearances of wealth and so ruin themselves," do you think that that is such an observation as an economist should take account of? If it is said: "Many people waste their capital by extravagant expenditure," do you think that that is an observation of which an economist should take account?

19. Do you think, as a matter of fact, that most people actually distribute their incomes in their expenditure so as to get the maximum of utility for themselves, judging by such standards of utility as they would admit to be sound when discussing the question of what things are useful abstractly? If there are many who do not do so, does that present a fact which the economist ought to take note of in his discussions?

Jevons, Theory, 76, 130–134.

20. Do you believe that there are crafty and able men who can "rig the market" and bull and bear prices more or less at their pleasure? Mention commodities with which this might be more possible than with others. Is it possible with stocks? If so, why? What should you say of such interferences on the whole and over a considerable period of time? Is the popular opinion correct about the extent to which manipulation of the market is possible?

Banker's Magazine, XXXVI., 308.

21. Was it the fundamental doctrine of the mercantile system that the precious metals are wealth exclusively or preëminently? If not, what was the fundamental doctrine of that system, and how was the doctrine just mentioned derived from it? Describe the development of the system.

Adam Smith, I., 15, Rogers's note; II., 63, Rogers's note. Cossa, 119, fg.

22. How was the colonial system a deduction from the mercantile system?

Adam Smith, II., 190–210.

23. Who were the Physiocrats and what did they teach?

Cossa, 142. Art. *Physiocrates* in the *Dictionnaire de l'Ec. Pol.*

24. Mention the leading English economists from Smith to J. S. Mill, giving dates and the chief contributions of each.

Cossa, 161–182. Life of Smith prefaced to Rogers's Smith.

II.

ELEMENTARY PRINCIPLES.

25. What is meant by a period of production? Show the great importance of observing the element of time in economic phenomena and correctly defining it in economic generalizations.

Jevons, Theory, 220–228.

26. What could supply and demand mean to Robinson Crusoe? When, in history, did supply and demand begin to act?

Supply and demand, at their lowest terms, are not a ratio, but a case of two simultaneous equations between two variables, or, they are represented by two curves which intersect. There are two persons and two commodities.—Prove this and show what errors must follow from treating supply and demand as a simple ratio.

How far can we analyze supply and demand?

Is the equilibrium of supply and demand accidental, imperfect, arbitrary, contingent, moral, or mathematical?

Jevons, Theory, Chap. IV.
Jenkin in Grant's Recess Studies, 151–171.
Princeton Review, November, 1882, p. 249–50

27. Effort and satisfaction are the pulsations by which the isolated man maintains existence. So soon as society exists division of labor begins and exchange follows. The systole and diastole of supply and demand are the form which the pulsations of effort and satisfaction take for a man who lives in society. Hence supply and demand are constant and all-pervading relations in society, and demand the first and most careful study of the economist.

Rights and obligations are the jurisprudential aspect of the relations of supply and demand.—Expand and criticise.

28. The law of supply and demand, in a free market without reserve, is that they come to an equilibrium at the ratio of value which will clear the market.—Compare Mill's law of the equation of international value and criticise the law here stated.

Mill, 358.

29. What is the difference between supply and demand and reciprocal demand?

Mill, 358. Cairnes' Principles, 89.

30. Value is a fact, not an opinion. It therefore has conditions of time and place, and may vary from moment to moment or place to place if successive sales take place.—Expand, illustrate, and establish, or refute, this statement.

31. "Value, economists are pretty much agreed, is a relation; and, for the purposes of the present discussion, we may so take it." A few pages further on: "Value is purchasing power; power in exchange." What further analysis is necessary to make these two definitions consistent?

Walker, Money and Trade, 30, 36.

32. "Wheat is worth 24 francs the hectolitre. This fact has the character of a natural fact. This value of wheat, reckoned in silver, does not result either from the will of the seller, or the will of the buyer, or from an agreement between them." "Wheat is worth 24 francs the hectolitre. This is a mathematical fact. The value of wheat in silver yesterday was 22 or 23 francs. A little while ago it was 23½ or 23¾. It will shortly be 24¼ or 24½. But to-day, at this instant, it is 24 francs, neither more nor less. This is a mathematical fact and admits of mathematical expression."—Explain and prove.

Walras, 29, 30.

33. If the supply of all commodities were doubled or halved suddenly, would any changes in their relative value ensue or not? (M. 774.)

Jevons, Theory, 142–155.

34. On the Black Friday of 1869 gold was sold on one side of the gold room for 160 when it was being sold on the other side for 135. Those on one side of the room knew a minute sooner than those on the other side that the Secretary of the Treasury had ordered five million dollars gold to be sold, adding so much to the supply.—How does this illustrate the doctrine of value? Cf. question 30.

35. Is either one of the following things commensurable; if so, which? Cost, desire, utility, satisfaction. What is "cost" according to Cairnes?

Cairnes, Principles, 73–87.

36. Why does not skill enter into cost? Is the fact here analogous to the fact that the rent of land does not enter into the price of agricultural produce?

Cairnes, Principles, 76–80.

37. Translate into English, *prix de revient.*

38. It is commonly said that value, in the long run, conforms to "cost of production." Jevons says: "I hold labor to be essentially variable, so that its value must be determined by the value

of the produce, not the value of the produce by that of labor." "Labor once spent has no influence on the future value of any article." He defines labor "all exertion of body or mind" by which we get products, and he says that it is incommensurable. Cairnes defines "cost" as all onerous exertion and sacrifice necessary to get goods. Macleod denies that labor produces value. He says that value produces or calls out labor. Sidgwick objects to Cairnes's use of "cost" that Cairnes spoke of the proportion of cost of production, but that we cannot think of "anything being in proportion to an aggregate of incommensurables." Marshall recognizes two uses of cost of production, adopts Cairnes's notion, and proposes the term "expenses of production" for the outlay, to which, as he and others say, normal value must conform.—Is Sidgwick's objection valid? Compare the above views and say whether the two senses of cost of production should be recognized, or, if only one, which?

Mill, 274–277. Jevons, Theory, 159–160.
Sidgwick, 201. Macleod, Econ. Philos., I., 331.

39. Jevons says that "Labor once spent has no influence on the future value of any article." On the wages system, if the labor spent last week was paid for by capital then consumed by the laborer, can value to be received ever have any effect back upon labor expended? or value be made to conform to capital formerly laid out? If we say that we shall make a new adjustment, in the next period of production, if we fail to replace our capital, will not the next period of production have all its own facts, circumstances and relations, and be, in fact, a new and independent problem?

40. Cost of production is a comparison of ratios. Cost is incommensurable, but the subject of it compares the cost with the satisfaction obtained. This ratio he cannot measure. It could not be measured and compared for two men, but the first man can compare the cost to him and the satisfaction to him in one line with the cost to him and the satisfaction to him in another, and this is what is really essential and is really done so long as two or more lines are open. Hence cost of production redistributes labor and capital and acts on supply; so ultimately on value. In no other way does it act on value, which is controlled by supply and demand only.—Criticise this doctrine. Suppose that no second line is open, and that the ratio of satisfaction to effort falls, as when a laborer advanced in life has to compete with a machine which lowers the price of his product, what happens then? and what becomes of the notion of cost of production as an ultimate regulator of value? What light does this last supposition throw on the last two questions?

41. "All other organs, therefore, jointly and individually, compete for blood with each organ, so that, though the welfare of each is indirectly bound up with that of the rest, yet, directly, each is antagonistic to the rest." "Evidently this process [of enlargement of an industry or development of a district whose products are in unusual demand] in each social organ, as in each individual organ, results from the tendency of the units to absorb all they can from the common stock of materials for sustentation; and evidently the resulting competition, not between units simply, but between organs, causes in a society, as in a living body, high nutrition and growth of parts called into greatest activity by the requirements of the rest."

Explain the doctrine of the first sentence and show how it applies to society. What light is here thrown on competition as a mode of growth, and on the general laws of life of which competition is one phase?

Spencer's Principles of Sociology, I., 535–6.

42. Criticise the expression "division of labor." Explain social organization. Show that division of labor is only a case of it. Show the power and utility of organization. What is proved in regard to the social and industrial utility of concord and peace? What is the law of the "Increasing Return?"

Marshall, Chap. VII., p. 57.

43. "Are the following to be included in capital? (1) the original powers of the laborer; (2) his acquired powers; (3) the original properties of the soil; (4) improvements on land; (5) credit; (6) unsold stock in the hands of a merchant; (7) articles purchased but still in the consumer's hands." (M. 166.)

Jevons, Theory, 245–253. Sidgwick, 120–141.

44. The savings of the United States have been estimated at 850 millions of dollars a year. What sort of things are these savings and where are they? (M. 177.)

Price, 113–14. Marshall, 15.

45. Capital is transmuted in every period of production. Prove this. Show its relation to "risk," and to any sound doctrine of wages.

Show that industry is limited by capital.

Mill, 39–41, 44.

46. The socialists declare that capital is produced (1) by accumulating the differences between buying price and selling price, i. e. the profits of merchants, and (2) by accumulating the differences between product and capital distributed to laborers. They regard the product as due entirely to labor, and therefore denounce the latter difference as an abstraction from the laborer of what belongs to him. They therefore construe the history of the last five hundred years as a period in which the middle class has developed itself by the accumulation of capital, (i. e. the plunder of the proletariat) and the creation of a capitalist system of industry. They construe civil liberty as the license given by the state to the robbery mentioned, and denounce competition as the mode in which the robbery is accomplished.

State what facts in the industrial history of the last five hundred years are here misconstrued, show the misconstruction, and put the facts in their true light.

Give an outline of the history of capital. When did it begin to be?

Describe the modern industrial system as compared with the system in England in the thirteenth century.

Cunningham, especially 139, 249. Seebohm.
Adam Smith, I., 273, Rogers's note. Walker, Land, 188.

47. Mention as many natural monopolies as you can. State when and why space, light, air, and water have value. Do honesty and truth have value? If so, why? Are natural monopolies beneficent or maleficent to man? Illustrate.

48. If fresh meat has hitherto been wasted in Australia and Buenos Ayres, and if refrigerator ships can be constructed which can carry that meat to Europe, what effects can you trace on the prices of certain commodities, on the distribution and increase of population, and on international competition in industry as likely to be produced?

Adam Smith, I., 245.

49. What is a speculator? Is he a parasite on the commercial system? If he performs a service, what is it? Is it a correct definition to say that he is one who bets on variations in prices?

Cairnes, Principles, 109. Adam Smith, II., 89 note, 199.
Nation, VII., 85.

50. Can we ever become too rich? Has the work to be done any limits? Is the work to be done a positive quantity? Does it remain constant?

Cairnes, Principles, 256–7.

51. "As the washing of clothes is not a productive industry, and its cost is one of the charges of living, it is an object that it should occasion as little drain upon the pecuniary resources of the community as possible."

Criticise the distinction between productive and unproductive labor.

52. Would it be a good state of things if no man could be found who would black another man's shoes for less than a dollar? Suppose, first, that all were proud and shiftless, and then make other suppositions.

53. "Discuss the effects of the exportation of capital (1) from England, (2) from Ireland." (M. 219.)

54. Can you assign any meaning to "over-production" in any case whatever.

Jevons, Theory, 190.

55. A cause of industrial depression was said to be "that the power to consume has not kept pace with the power to produce. It is not the fault of the power of production, [i. e., it is not over production.] It is a fault on the other side."

If production should exceed consumption, what would become of the difference? If consumption should exceed production, where would we get the difference?

Cairnes, Principles, 31-36.

56. What are the economic objections to gambling?

Cf. Jevons, 154. Spencer, Study of Sociology, 306.

57. In a certain city a piece of grading was to be done. It was known and admitted that it would cost 15 cents per cubic foot to do it by contract and 45 cents per foot to do it by days labor. Some favored doing it the latter way and replied to the objection of greater cost that there would be no loss or injury to the interest of the city because the money would be paid to laborers resident in the city, and so would stay there.—Show the fallacy of this reasoning.

58. Suppose that, in consequence of great reduction in the cost of transportation between the United States and England, the gains of agriculture in England should greatly decline, what would be the successive stages of effect, and what the ultimate effect on the wealth of England, and why? (M. 38.) What would be the effect in the United States?

59. What is the value of the obelisk in the Central Park? Its first cost to its modern owner was 0. It cost $100,000 to move it and set it up.
Jevons, Theory, 159.

60. A one dollar bank note is in circulation, which is a counterfeit, but no one has detected it. What is its value?

The promoters of a stock company, by puffing it in the newspapers, have run the stock up to 150. What is the value of it?

A false bottom was put into an elevator bin so that it held 50 bushels when it was supposed to hold 10,000. What was the effect on the market price of wheat? What was the value of wheat?

A piece of cloth was sold for all wool for $1.00 a yard. It contained 10 per cent. cotton. What was its value?

A grocer tampered with his scales so that he sold 15 ounces for a pound. He charged "10 cts. a pound" for sugar. What was the value of sugar?

61. A piece of land was owned by 15 persons. Desiring to divide without selling it, they employed three real estate experts to divide it into 15 parts which should be of equal value. This was done. The next year the tax assessors assessed the 15 shares at amounts varying from $900 to $2,850.

What light does this incident throw on value?

62. In 1870 a house was built which cost $100,000. In 1876 it was appraised in an estate at $75,000 because that was judged to be what it would sell for. In 1880 it was sold for $150,000. There were those who claimed in 1876 that it should be appraised at what it cost in 1870, or at what it would sell for in 1880 so far as they could then foresee that. What do you say?

63. What causes determine the market value of oysters?

Cairnes, Principles, 141–146.

64. "Suppose a considerable rise in the price of wool to be foreseen, how should farmers expect the prices of mutton, beef and hides, respectively to be affected, and why?" (M. 868.)

65. The Dutch East India Co. used to destroy part of the spice crop in order to enhance its profits. Was there a fallacy in the proceeding? (M. 547.)

Adam Smith, II., 101.

III.

POPULATION.

66. Population increases up to the limit of the sustaining power of the land at a given stage of the arts and under a given standard of living, or, mortality and reproduction are equal at the limit, on a given stage of the arts, and with a given standard of living.—Explain and prove this law.

Spencer, Biology, II., 479. Cairnes, Logical Method, 149–181.
Roscher, II., 273–336. Mill, 96–100.
Fawcett, Pauperism, Chap. III.

67. What is over-population? What is under-population? British India has 200 to the square mile; Belgium, 469; Rhode Island, 254. Which comes nearer to over-population and which to under-population?

Roscher, II., 337–341.

68. How is the ratio Land : Population affected by advance in the arts and higher standard of living?

Adam Smith, I., 262.

69. The law of population and the law of the diminishing return show that, other things being constant, the human race, in the process of time, must advance towards misery, pestilence, famine and war. State in detail what "the other things" are? Are they constant? If they vary, what makes them do so? Define civilization from this point of view. Show what produces civilization; what it consists of; what its effects are. Do any of your facts or deductions bring out "exceptions" to the laws of population and the diminishing return, or prove those laws untrue?

Princeton Review, November, 1881, p. 303.

70. What is the importance for land rent, wages, rate of interest, and so for the status of the population, of the ratio Land : Population? What is the limit of that ratio?

71. Make a complete catalogue of food-plants and discuss their comparative economic value.

IV.

LAND AND RENT.

72. Discuss the following definitions of rent:

"Rent is that portion of the produce of the earth which is paid to the landlord for the use of the original and indestructible powers of the soil."

Rent is the price paid for the use of an appropriated natural monopoly.

Ricardo, 34. Walker, 203. McCulloch's Adam Smith, 444. Adam Smith, I., 151, Rogers's note.

73. State the law of the diminishing return. Mention as many things as you can to which it applies. Why do we find our population scattered sparsely over our whole territory and not concentrated on the Atlantic coast? Why is American agriculture slovenly? Why have our agricultural colleges obtained few students of the science of agriculture? Why is forestry neglected in the United States? Why are we not a pains taking people? Why are we not frugal?

Marshall, 21–26. Walker, Land, 45–6.

74. If the land of a certain district constituting an economic unit (i. e. such that, with existing means of transportation, no staples of food could profitably be brought into it) were all of a uniform quality, would none of it bear rent?

Adam Smith, I., 151–169, with Rogers's notes.

75. A court has been established in Ireland to adjust rents between landlord and tenant. Is this the same thing as fixing wages or prices by some public authority?

Cairnes, Essays, 202–231.

76. It is argued that the system of "judicial rents" will produce two sets of landlords instead of one. What is the argument? Is it sound? It is argued that fifteen years hence another equally arbitrary interference with contract will be necessary. What is the ground of that argument?

77. Can a class of peasant proprietors be brought into existence by any legislative machinery?

78. What are the social and economic objections to the French system for the inheritance of

land? What are the objections to the English custom of settlements?

Mill, 540. Edinburgh Review, XL., 350.
Nation, XV., 218; XX., 312.
Probyn, 122–126; 184–212, cf. 108; 291–312.
Brodrick, 129–151. Walker, Land, 212 fg. Letourneau, 440.

79. Discuss historically and logically this thesis: The tenure of land of the tiller of the soil is always most fixed where personal independence is lowest, and, the more liberty and individualism are developed, the more precarious is the tenure of land.—At what point does fixity of tenure turn from the bondage of the villain to the blessing of the free man?

Cunningham, 54, 97, 111, 197–199. Seebohm, 176–178.

80. Do you know of any place where the "margin of cultivation" or the "Ricardian acre" can be seen? Where would you look for it? Does it contravene the Ricardian law of rent to show that the "margin of cultivation" for England is in the United States?

81. "Few Irish farms have been able to furnish the family of the actual cultivator with a comfortable subsistence, and leave something over to be contributed to the support of another family in a certain ease. In England, owing to a greater abundance of capital, and the existence of manufactures, the landlord has been compelled to put up with a smaller share, because the farmer's standard of living was higher, and his traditions of comfort and respectability so strong, that no landlord could compel him to lower them in order to pay a greater rent."

82. Definition of a fair rent: "A rent which might be fairly paid, and yet permit a tenant not deficient in those qualities of industry and providence which are expected in any walk of life to live and thrive."

83. Is there any rent on a fishery, or a quarry? Is there any rent on a water power? Is stumpage a kind of rent? Is there any rent on a mine? Note Rogers's comment (Adam Smith, I., 177), and test his doctrine by the facts of the coal trade in the United States.

Adam Smith, I., 171–185. Mill, 288.

84. If one man owned New York harbor could he obtain rent for it? How great would the rent be? What now becomes of what he would get?

85. "How are pasture rents, shooting rents, and ground rents of dwellings determined respectively?" (M. 643.)

86. A picture by a great artist and an acre of land sold in 1825 for the same price. In 1875 the same picture and the same acre changed hands again for ten times as much each. Is there any reason why the state should sequestrate all the increased value ("unearned increment") in one case and not in the other? (M. 725.)

87. It is said that a publisher pays Mr. Tennyson £4,000 per annum for the exclusive right to publish everything written by Mr. T. Is there here anything analogous to rent? If any analogy, how far imperfect?

88. A manager pays a prima donna so much for each evening's performance. How far is there here any analogy to rent?

89. What are *latifundia?* Where can we see *latifundia* to-day, or the nearest resemblance to them?

Letourneau, 424.

90. Discuss the proposition that the United States shall sell no more land without reserving the right to demand in future years the unearned increment. Hitherto the popular land policy in the United States has been that the land should be given away freely, or at a nominal price, to actual settlers. Has this been a mistake? What is the fact about the tenure of land in the theory of American law as compared with the same in the theory of English law?

Sumner, Jackson, 184–191.

91. Under what head would you classify the income of a patentee or an author; wages, profits, or rent? (M. 23.)

92. Write an essay on Village Communities.

Maine, Village Communities; De Lavelaye, Primitive Property; Seebohm, the English Village Community; Wallace, Russia.

V.

WAGES.

93. Mention as many different ways as you know of, in which labor has received, or does receive, remuneration for its share in production.

94. Obviously it is necessary, in order to understand the operation of the industrial system, to trace the steps of one action and reaction with care and detail. But production, exchange, distribution, and consumption, production, exchange, etc., follow each other in a never ending series. They in fact overlap at consumption and production, as when the laborer, his energies revived by sleep and breakfast, takes up his spade and again tills the ground. It is in distribution, however, that the replacement of the capital takes place, and we must begin to study a complete reaction either with consumption or production. It really is immaterial, save that our point of cessation must correspond with our point of beginning. If we follow through one reaction, we shall find that it will cover the consumption, transmutation, and replacement of the capital and a distribution and adjustment of it to begin a new enterprise.—Criticise.

95. Wages are the remuneration of labor.

Wages are the sum paid per unit of time by the employer to the employee, in return for which the employee contracts to employ his productive energy during a specified time in such manner as the employer may direct.

Criticise these definitions.

Cf. Adam Smith, I., 67, 69.

96. Describe in detail the contract or competitive wages system as a part of the modern industrial system, and show what the relations of employer and employee and their mutual rights and duties are in it. Who constitute the wages class? Is there any distinctly differentiated wages class in the United States? Under what circumstances is such a class distinctly differentiated?

Walker, Pol. Econ., 379.
Stirling in Grant's Recess Studies, 309–333.
Jenkin, ibid., 171–187.

97. Cairnes argues that we cannot apply the law of supply and demand to labor, because the supply of labor is produced by biological forces and not as commodities are produced.—What is the fallacy of this argument?

Cairnes, Principles, 152–3.

98. If a change takes place in the supply of labor, will a *proportionate* change take place in wages? (Cf. question 33.)

Rogers, Prices, I., 265, 275.

99. An author who defines wages as the share of labor in the product, writes: "The *industrial* conditions were more favorable to the payment of wages in the United States, while in England the *financial* conditions were more favorable." Does he violate his definition? What is the force of the antithesis in the italicized words?

100. Mill (p. 145 and again p. 207, end of chap. X.) speaks of the laborers as one of the classes amongst whom the *product* is divided. At the beginning of chap. XI. and afterwards, he says that wages are paid out of *capital*. Is there an inconsistency here? If so, what is the cause of it, and how is it to be solved? Does he use two different definitions of "wages"?

Cf. also pp. 430–439.

Princeton Review, November, 1882, p. 251.

101. Sidgwick (p. 318), commenting on the confusion between product and capital noticed in the last question, says: "This confusion seems to be best avoided by considering the assistance to production rendered by labor—whatever form it may take—as constituting the real capital of the employer who purchases it; and the commodities that continually pass into the consumption of the laborers as their share of the produce."—Criticise this proposition. Note that "assistance" is said to be capital, and the assistance of the employee to be the capital of the employer.

102. Sidgwick says again (same page): "The employer purchases the result of a week's labor, which thereby becomes a part of his capital; and may be conceived, if we omit for simplicity's sake the medium of exchange, to give the laborer in return some of the finished product of his industry."—Criticise this view.

103. "As the employer generally makes a profit, the payment of wages is, so far as he is concerned, but the return to the laborer of a portion of the capital he has received from the labor: so far as the employee is concerned, it is but the receipt of a portion of the capital his labor has previously produced." How does this doctrine differ from that in the last question?

104. It is held that the laborer is the residual claimant of the product of industry after rent, profits, and wages of superintendence have been paid out of it.—Criticise this doctrine. How, under this doctrine or that of the last three questions, would you account for the great advance in wages and other remuneration of labor after the great Plague of 1348?

Walker, Pol. Econ., 265. Adam Smith, I., 109, Rogers's note.
Cunningham, 188-195. Rogers, Prices, I., 265.

105. Sidgwick says (p. 322): "What remains after subtracting the aggregate price paid for the use of capital (including land) is obviously the share of labor in the aggregate."—Criticise that doctrine. How would this and the doctrine of the last question differ from the old doctrine that wages and profits are the leavings of each other?

106. Competitive or contract wages and profits are in no sense the leavings of each other. They are not parts of the same whole. The wages come out of capital. Hence one who has no capital of his own, or borrowed, can not become an employer, however great a chance of profit he may see. The profits come out of the product. The two (capital and product) stand, one before and the other after the transmutation of capital which occurs in every period of production, and they are as distinct as the plowman's dinner in April and the farmer's sheaf in August, or as the tailor's coat which he is wearing and the employer's coat which the tailor is making. The complementary parts of capital are raw material and fixed capital. The wages enter into the product, not as an explicit, but an implicit, arithmetical factor. The product consists of the replacement of the capital, profits, and rent. The replacement of the capital consists of wages, raw material, and wear of fixed capital. Hence we get two equations, letting x = wages and t=profits: $x+y+z$=capital; $(x+y+\frac{z}{m})+t+u$= product. Capital and product bear no known relation to each other. Hence no ratio of x to t can possibly be derived, although it is plain that an increase of x, other factors remaining constant, would be unfavorable to t.—Expand and criticise.

Mill, 20, 35, 37. Cairnes, Principles, 159–180.
Walker, Pol. Econ., 380.

107. Wages do not belong in distribution at all. They belong under the head of consumption —productive consumption of capital carried forward and constantly re-applied, from one period of production to another, to sustain society and increase the power of man over nature. Hence the doctrine that wages are paid out of capital is alone consistent with any sound knowledge of the evolution of industry and the growth of society. If we treat economics under two heads, statics and dynamics, discarding the old divisions as unphilosophical, wages will fall in the department of dynamics. They are the tie which unites two parties in the application of capital to production, viz: one who wants to live by the increase of his capital and cannot do so without productive effort; the other, who wants to live by productive effort but cannot do so, in a highly organized society, without capital. Hence the two motives unite them in a contract relation whose general aim is their common interest, but within which their interests are antagonistic. Hence nothing can benefit either which (like limiting production) is hostile to their common interest, and, under free competition, if either of them wins a temporary advantage over the other, he will have to pay it back again with interest, but probably to the net advantage of both. Hence their antagonism, if carried out by legitimate means, is the law of life and growth and not an evil at all. Cf. question 41.—Criticise this doctrine.

108. "The capital of the employer is, by no means, the real source of the wages of even the workmen employed by him. It is only the immediate reservoir through which wages are paid out, until the purchasers of the commodities produced by that labor make good the advance and thereby encourage the undertaker to purchase additional labor."—Show the fallacy. Is "reservoir" a valid analogy? Suppose that the product found no purchasers, or was burned up?

Roscher, II., 56.

109. Macleod, whose fundamental proposition is that "credit is capital," argues that wages are paid in credit, i. e. that the employer pays his laborers with bank notes. These notes "have been part of the 'wages-fund' and have been 'capital' exactly as if they had been sovereigns." "Hence we see that not only the accumulation of past profits is brought into the wages-fund, but also the anticipation of future profits. * * Every future profit has a present value, and that present value may be brought into the 'wages-fund' and made 'capital' of."—Criticise the use of credit, capital, and money in this argument. Show that on this argument only, if it should be admitted, would it be true that wages can come out of product.

Macleod, II., 120–128.

110. If an industry was generally depressed, but one employer was, by exception, making high profits, what rate of wages would he pay? If an industry was highly prosperous, but one employer was, by exception, making no profits, what rate of wages would he pay?

Princeton Review, November, 1882, p. 255.

111. Is it the same thing to say that wages are determined by the supply and demand of labor, and that wages are determined by the ratio of capital available for wages to laborers ready to work?

Mill, 207. Princeton Review, November, 1882, p. 259.

112. What is the effect of an increased demand for commodities on the wages fund?

Cairnes, Principles, 194-200.

113. What is the relation between prices of products and wages of the laborers who make those products?

Mill, 208-211. Cairnes, Principles, 200-210.
Rogers, Prices, IV., 491.

114. What is the fallacy of connecting wages by a sliding scale with the price of the product?

Marshall, 216.

115. If the intervals at which wages are paid are longer than the period of production in any industry, are the wages paid out of product, or is the employer swindling the employee? If the latter, show how.

116. Cairnes teaches that the capital is divided, at the beginning of the period of production, into

fixed capital, raw material, and wages fund. Later he argues that, if trades unions could succeed in putting up wages, they would reduce profits so low as to check accumulation.—Show the inconsistency and show where the error lies.

Princeton Review, November, 1882, p. 252.

117. What is the effect to be expected on the wages of laborers from insurance against accident, sickness, or death, (1) if the employers pay for it in whole or in part; (2) if "the state" pays for it in whole or in part?

Fawcett, Pol. Econ., 6th Ed., Chap. XI.

118. It is said that the gains of the venturer (wages of superintendence) are analogous to rent. What ground is there for this opinion? Is the venturer the landlord, the farmer, or the land?

Walker, Pol. Econ., 247–255. Mill, 290.

119. If the land of Great Britain should be confiscated, would the wages of any employments be affected? If so, which ones, and why?

120. If trades unions should establish a rule that women should have the same wages as men wherever they are employed in similar work, would that rule be for the benefit of women or of men?

121. Suppose that working time should be reduced 20 per cent., what would be the effect on real wages, on profits, and on prices? Compare scarcity-high-wages with plenty-high-wages.

Cf. Rogers, Prices, IV., 491.

122. "The maintenance of a standard of comfort among laborers is like the maintenance of a sea wall; if a section give way all defense is lost. Examine how far this is true, and investigate the limits of defensible rules that laborers as a body may impose on their associates." (M. 409.)

To what extent have trades union rules aimed at or attained the end of maintaining the standard of comfort?

123. Do you think that the protective taxes lower the standard of living of American wage receivers?

124. Strikes and trades union rules do not have equal chances of success in all trades. Their chances are better according as the trade is a monopoly on account of physical circumstances, or special training, or skill, and according as the public is annoyed by any interruption of the industry.—Prove this.

Thornton, 340–360. Marshall, 187–198. Price, Chap. VIII. Sumner, What Classes Owe, Chap. VI.

125. Is there any ground for believing that struggles between employers and employees can be done away with by arbitration? Can arbitration be employed in the making of a contract or is it confined to the interpretation of a contract?

Marshall, 214–217.

126. Is it for the advantage of the wages class to find some new and cheaper article of diet?

Is it for the advantage of the wages class that the wives and children of men of that class should work for wages?

Is it a sign of advance in the community when we see more boys employed as cash boys, messengers, etc.?

Adam Smith, I., 76, 168–170. Mill, 242.
Walker, Pol. Econ., 321. McCulloch's Adam Smith, 467.

127. What is the effect on wages of having part of the population soldiers, pensioners, paupers and convicts, or an undue proportion of them priests, monks and civil servants? Are not such persons withdrawn from competition in the labor supply? How does your answer bear on the question whether convicts ought to be employed or kept idle?

The farmers of the United States are told that it is for their interest to pay protective taxes to support manufactures, because otherwise the manufacturing population would all compete in agriculture. What is the fallacy of this argument? Connect your answer to this question with the answer to the last?

Sumner, Argument, etc., 7.

128. Discuss briefly the employment of convicts, in its economic aspects; discriminate the cases where they are employed under superintendents, or on a contract system; at the market price or below; all in one trade, or in a number of trades.

Mill, 240–241.

129. Can the landowners of Great Britain take all the advantage of the natural deposits of coal and metal in that country, and not let British wage receivers have a share in the bounty of nature to their country?

Cairnes, Principles, 54–57.

130. What is the effect on wages and profits of exporting capital?

Can any connection be traced between the exportation of capital and the migration of labor?

Suppose that English capital builds a railroad

in Iowa and an English laborer migrates to Iowa, settles on the railroad line, and cultivates land. What are the economic effects on all the parties interested, and on the wealth of the two countries?

Adam Smith, II., 216, Rogers's note.

131. What is "store-pay?" Show by an analysis of the transaction why it is very injurious to wage receivers. Do the phenomena of store-pay throw any light for the economist on contract wages?

132. An American landowner is often also a mechanic; say, for instance, a carpenter. He builds a barn for some one and agrees to take his pay in a lump sum when the barn is done. What is the economic analysis of such a case? Does it throw any light on the theory of wages?

133. How would the economist describe in the technical language of his science that which the popular dialect describes as "living from hand to mouth?" Describe any persons in savage or civilized life who so live? Can any inferences as to a sound wages system be drawn from the phenomena of living from hand to mouth?

134. "A high rate of wages indicates, not a high, but a low cost of production for all commodities measured in which the wages are high." —Prove this.

Cairnes, Principles, 382–386.

135. "Show how a rise or fall of the average rate of wages within a country acts on its external trade." (M. 435.)

Cairnes, Principles, 318–341.

136. "In the island of Laputa a law was passed compelling each workman to work with his left hand tied behind his back, and the law was justified on the ground that the demand for labor was more than doubled by it. Examine this argument." (M. 443.) Would the human race be better off on earth if each person had only one arm? If a race should be evolved which had four arms, would it be doomed to misery and extinction?

137. Some coal-workers want a diminution of the out-put of coal as a means of keeping up their wages. How far, if at all, would the means accomplish the end? (M. 444.) Would the human race be better off if the richness of the existing deposits of coal was reduced ten per cent.?

138. "The day-laborer, feeling himself more of a man than formerly, must oftener wear a white laundered shirt, but he cannot pay over 50 cents for one. The demand of the higher civilization of the day-laborer must be met, and white laundered shirts are supplied at retail for 50 cents or even for 37 cents. But the wages of the women who make them have been reduced to 8 cents per shirt."—Show the fallacy. Can a man raise his standard of living at the expense of others, just because he wants to? Does true rise in the standard of living of one lower the wages of others?

139. In a shoe town a retail shoe-dealer undersells all his competitors 25 cents per pair. He "obtains from the manufacturer his lowest price for making 100 cases as per sample. He then offers to pay so much—a sum less than the manufacturer's estimate—and pay cash. The manufacturer, rather than lose a good cash order, consents to make the goods, but not being able to reduce the cost of raw materials takes the discount out of labor."—Argued that the wages receivers work against themselves and each other by buying as cheaply as they can. Show the fallacy.

140. Ricardo said (p. 241): "In America and many other countries, where the food of man is easily provided, there is not nearly such great temptation to employ machinery as in England, where food is high, and costs much labor for its production."—Criticise this. What is the fact about the "temptation to employ" labor-saving machinery in the United States, and what is the reason for it?

141. Ricardo goes on: "The same cause that raises [the wages of] labor, [i. e. greater cost at which food is obtained for an increasing population] does not raise the value of machines, and, therefore, with every augmentation of capital, a greater proportion of it is employed on machinery."—Is the doctrine here laid down true? Is the reason given for it correct?

Cairnes, Principles, 174–180.

142. Define and illustrate industrial copartnership. Whence comes the gain by industrial copartnership? Is the principle capable of indefinite extension and application? If not, what are its limits? What permanent good will the plan accomplish, if it is generally employed? Why is it not popular with trades unionists?

Thornton, 363–397.

143. What are the reasons for the gain in coöperative stores? Is the principle of such stores capable of indefinite expansion and application? If not, what is the limit? What would result if coöperative stores should entirely displace private establishments? Will such stores produce a permanent improvement? If so, what will it be?

Thornton, 397–418

144. Coöperation in production and distribution aims to reduce or do away with wages of superintendence. Would this be a great gain? Is it possible?

Holyoake, II., 86.

145. By aiding and encouraging the accumulation of capital, coöperative stores operate a kind of natural selection on the non-capitalist class, selecting out those who have the will and energy to better themselves, and helping them on, while depressing by just so much more those who are shiftless. If the selected women marry only the selected men, the separation between these two sections of what was once one class widens from time to time.—Expand and prove this or refute it.

Holyoake, II., 193–4.

146. Having in mind your answer to the last question, discuss a proposition to provide decent lodgings for the miserable, by the interference of the municipality in a way involving expense to tax payers.

147. Using your answers to the last two questions, show which kind of schemes for social aid favor the survival of the fittest, and which kind favor the survival of the unfittest. Can any scheme have any other effect than one of these two?

148. What is the effect of free common schools on the comparative wages of skilled and unskilled laborers?

. What is the effect of free schools, including high schools, on the salary of female teachers?

What is the effect of endowed colleges and seminaries on the salary of clergymen?

What would be the effect of technical and industrial schools, maintained by taxation, on the wages of artisans?

Adam Smith, I., 136–142; II., 363, and Rogers's note.

149. "On what does the rate of interest depend? Is it affected by the amount of the currency? Does the rate of interest affect the price of land or stocks?" (M. 561; 565.)

Mill, 391. Jevons, Theory, 242–245.

VI.

CONSUMPTION.

150. The most important phenomenon in distribution, distinguishing distribution from consumption, is the replacement of the capital.—Expand and explain.

151. Show the need of investigating consumption as a department of political economy. Show that the proposition: a demand for commodities is not a demand for labor, is a guiding principle for a correct study of consumption.

152. Translate "A demand for commodities is not a demand for labor" into other and less technical terms in order to bring out its meaning.

153. At the end of a certain period of production A, B, C, D, etc., were each a creditor in the market for $1,000. A bought and took as his share that value in jewelry. B took means of subsistence and lived in idleness while consuming them. C took the same but distributed part amongst servants who served him while he was idle. D took the same and gave part to laborers who dug an ornamental lake in his grounds. E took the same and gave it to laborers who built a railroad which was not needed and could not pay working expenses. F took his partly in the same, partly in tools and seed, and employed laborers to produce a crop of corn. G took his in tools, etc., which were wanted by certain foreigners to whom he lent them on interest. Thus the second period of production passed. What was the effect of the course pursued by each of these men on the capital of the community in the third period of production, and on the interest of wage receivers in the second period and afterwards?

154. Show that "a demand for commodities is not, etc.," traverses the following fallacies:

(1) That the spendthrift is the benefactor of the wage receiver.

(2) That wages paid measure cost of production.

(3) That wages are or may be paid out of product.

(4) That trades-union rules benefit wage-receivers by "making work."

(5) That we "want work" when we want wages.

(6) That we need to take measures to "give a circulation to money."

(7) That we want "an industry" when we want goods.

Adam Smith, I., 343–353. Mill, 53. Marshall, 16.
Cairnes, Principles, 48–54; 194–196; 249; 254.

155. How do the things which are luxuries vary from time to time? What definiteness can be given to the notion of a luxury?

156. Is there any cause for anxiety on account of the large amount of "foreign luxuries" which are imported into the United States?

157. Luxurious consumption is selfish and unsocial; productive consumption causes activity in a great number and variety of social functions, and multiplies the active relations of the consumer with others.—Criticise this assertion.

158. Discuss the economic effects on a community of an increased expenditure for theatrical and similar entertainments.

159. What judgment is to be passed on "an idle rich man" who has no vices, regarding him and his behavior solely from the economic standpoint?

160. A writer on behalf of the Chinese in California estimates their earnings at fifteen million dollars, and then makes this argument to show the good they do to that State: "Of this sum, ten per cent. having been deducted for savings, thirteen and one-half million dollars will pass into general circulation, remaining to enrich the State, or passing out of it to pay the debts of the general population. It is a stream of wealth which enriches the whole region."—Did he properly use his facts to prove his case?

161. "Luzerne County contains an area of 1,350 square miles. Until the development of the coal trade, the agricultural production of the county was in excess of the home consumption. Now a different state of affairs exists. The rapid increase of population from 1860 to 1870, amounting to 90,000, changed the former order of things, and notwithstanding she contains within her limits some of the most fertile lands in the State, her agricultural productions now fall far short of the amount necessary for home consumption. Nearly one-half of her citizens are non-producers, relying upon the coal interest either directly or indirectly for their employment or support."

162. "If one-third of the present agricultural laborers in the (Western) States would become mechanics, miners, etc., and thus consumers of their former products, the other two-thirds would find no trouble in sending their diminished surplus to the East at reasonable rates, and would retain at home the money now sent abroad to purchase manufactured articles for their own consumption."

163. State the economic effects to all parties concerned, on the island and elsewhere, if a certain island, otherwise only sparsely populated, should become a sanitary resort.

164. An Irish landlord had an income from rent of £x For four years he kept up a certain establishment, hiring servants and buying supplies wherever he lived, and exchanging his surplus income entirely for products of France, i. e. wine, brandy, silks, laces, ribbons, etc. The first year he lived on his estate, the second in Dublin, the third in London, and the fourth in Paris. Was he an "absentee" in his second year? What was the effect on the wealth of France, England, or Ireland, or on the interests of any class in any one of these countries, of his changes in his place of living?

He then changed his policy. He kept up the same establishment and hired servants and bought supplies wherever he lived, as before, but he saved and made capital of his surplus. The first year he lived in Paris and invested his savings there. The next year he staid in Paris but sent all his savings to Ireland for investment. The third year he lived on his estate in Ireland and invested all his savings there. The fourth year he staid in Ireland, but sent all his savings to Paris for investment. What was the effect of his new policy in each of the four years on the wealth of France and Ireland, and on the interests of any class in either?

165. A owns some land, some railroad stock and a share in a factory, in Colorado. Does the ownership of either of these pieces of property create a duty for him to live in Colorado; if so, of which?

Is there any class in Colorado for whose interest it is that he should live there? If so, what class?

166. Would you say that a man might live anywhere on earth that he chose, undisturbed by the fear lest he was doing wrong, or neglecting his duty to some of his fellow men, by living in one place rather than another? If not, modify the statement as you think necessary.

Would it make any difference with your answer whether you regarded the feudal relations of landlord and tenant as entirely superseded by contract relations, or not?

167. "We are glad to see this determination among millionaires not to be outdone by one another [in building expensive steam yachts]. It is a rivalry in which all take the greatest interest, and by which all are indirectly benefited." "Extravagance, when practiced by millionaires is a blessed thing. It causes a freer circulation of money, affords the laboring man work, feeds women and children, and affects, in fact, every industry, no matter how small."

168. "There was a notion that the money appropriated by the river and harbor bill was thrown away. Where? Probably ninety per cent. went into muscle and labor."

169. Suppose that, by a change in climate, the household consumption of coal in the United States should be reduced one-half, what would be the effect on the wealth of the country? (M. 36.)

170. Suppose that we should succeed in producing a horse-power by electricity at one-half the cost of producing the same by steam, what

would be the immediate and what the ultimate effect on the wealth of the country? and on particular parts of its wealth?

171. Describe the state of society which would be produced if, as fast as capital was accumulated, it was put to productive employment, none of it being consumed luxuriously, and if this was kept up for, say, fifty years.

VII.

MONEY, CURRENCY AND BANKING.

172. Money is any commodity which is set apart by common consent to serve as a medium of exchange. Analyze and justify, or criticise and correct this definition.

173. Is money a measure of value? If so, why not include another specification in the definition? Define carefully "a measure of value." It has been objected that value is a ratio (*e.g.*, ¾) and that we cannot measure a ratio. Is that objection valid? Is money a "denominator of value?" Does "denominator of value" cover all that is correct and essential in "measure of value?"

McCulloch's Adam Smith, 480 fg., and Art. Money in the Encyc. Britan. 8th ed.

174. Currency is a collective term for all forms of credit instruments by which the use of the medium of exchange (money) is dispensed with, the instruments of credit serving as records and evidence of the rights of the parties until such time as value may be given and received for value. Instruments of credit are not a cheap kind of money. There is no such thing as cheap money. Instruments of credit are not in any sense "substitutes for money," or "representatives of money."—Explain and criticise this definition. Test it in the case of bank-notes, checks, promissory notes, book debts.

175. In barter, one thing is given for another. In the money system, one thing is given for money and money is given for the other. In the credit system, the instruments of credit are not "media of exchange." One thing is given as half of a barter, and a credit instrument (transferable or not) is created as a record and evidence of the fact, and of a debt. When the other thing is given the barter is concluded and the evidence of debt is cancelled. The utility of credit is that it makes money unnecessary.—Criticise and explain. Show why, as credit becomes more general, the function of money as a measure of value becomes more and more important.

176. Show that, historically, money was first invented and used as a measure of value; that, in time, when the "money system" had superseded barter, the function of money as a medium oi exchange came to predominate; that the function of measure of value is now again becoming the more important as credit institutions are developed.

177. "Of the money daily used a very small percentage is bank-notes. The great bulk is checks, drafts and telegrams. The telegraph transmits millions upon millions of bank credits from Boston to New York, Chicago, London, etc., etc., and the reverse, where the telegram is the only money used." If, instead of telegraphing, a man should telephone, would his words be money? In the contribution box in church were specie, greenbacks and bank-notes. A gentleman put in his card with $1.00 written in the corner. If the greenbacks and bank-notes were money, was the card money? A play-writer, being under personal obligation to an actor sent him a card on which was written, "Good for a three-act comedy." Was this card money, if greenbacks and bank-notes are money? Is any definition of money possible if it goes beyond the selected commodity?

178. How would the question, whether Clearing House Certificates are money or not, affect or be affected by different definitions of money?

179. A public-house keeper gave a glass of beer to a shoemaker and put a chalk-mark on the door against the shoemaker's name. After a certain time the shoemaker made and delivered to the landlord a pair of shoes, thereby cancelling the score. Was the chalk-mark money? Was it currency? Suppose that the shoemaker had sold the shoes for a bank-note and paid his score with the note, would the note be money? Would it be currency? Would the chalk-mark then be money? Or currency? Suppose that the landlord gave a receipt for the payment, would that be money? Would it be currency? What criticism do these questions suggest on the definition that money is any medium of exchange?

180. Show the fallacy of any definition of money which puts checks in one category and bank-notes in another. Is it a correct criterion to say that bank-notes are taken in "final" payment, or "without recourse?"

Walker, Money, 399.

181. "Credit, no doubt, is a comparatively fragile and perishable instrument for transferring wealth." The "credit" of a banker who is barely solvent, if solvent at all, is said to be part of the capital of the bank, "provided we are careful to point out that such capital is of fragile nature, liable to sudden destruction in case of a panic."—Criticise the notions of credit, capital and medium of exchange. Note especially "fragile."

Sidgwick, 129, 239.

182. Define depreciation and appreciation of the currency. What causes may produce either? What are the effects of either?

More generally, what determines the value of the currency?

Hertzka, 20–76; 192–224. Chevalier on Gold, 124–137.
Cairnes, Essays, 53–77.

183. Define carefully the effect of habit in regard to money.

184. State the law of the distribution of the precious metals.

Walker, Money, Chap. III.

185. A coin is a piece of metal convenient for circulation which is assayed for quality, weighed for quantity, and stamped by authority as a guarantee of weight and fineness.—Expand and explain. Is a coin a highly developed tool? Sketch the history of coins.

Art. Coinage, in Lalor's Cyclopedia.

186. Some say that gold and silver are plainly indicated by Providence as the materials for money; others say that we use gold for money only because it is the most convenient thing we know of for the purpose. Which do you think right?

187. If we work a gold mine, gold comes out. What goes in? On what does it depend whether the community gains or loses by the exchange?

Adam Smith, I., 184; II., 141–4.
Cairnes, Essays, 43–52.

188. What facts go to determine the amount of money which a country needs?

Mill, 306. Roscher I., 366–374. Chevalier III., 615–650.
Walker, Money, 44–76.

189. May an English cobbler get gold at less cost than a California miner?

Mill, 366–369. Cairnes, Essays, 103. Roscher, I., 378–380.

190. In what respect is it an advantage to get gold first after it leaves the mines? What was the effect on Spain of being the first through whose hands the gold of America passed in the sixteenth century?

Adam Smith, I., 199; II., 86–88. Cairnes, Essays, 93–108.
Cairnes, Principles, 412–14.

191. One nation having conquered another in war forced it to pay a great war indemnity. Trace the effects on capital, money, prices, wages, profits and credit in each country.

Price, 380–382.

192. France paid to Germany over a thousand million dollars. What were the actual transactions by which this payment was made? Analyze those transactions and show their significance in an economic or financial point of view.

Say, 195. Giffen, Chap. I.

193. The mint price of gold, .900 fine, at the San Francisco and Philadelphia mints is $18.604. Why then is gold ever shipped from California to New York? (M. 990.)

194. Give the history of the trade dollar? What was the object aimed at by the coin when first coined? Was it a desirable object, and was coining the trade dollar a good means of accomplishing it? What is now the difficulty and danger connected with the trade dollar? What legal ground of obligation exists, if any, why the United States should redeem those coins at par in gold?

195. We read in the money article, "The price for silver bullion in London is $50\frac{15}{16}$ pence per ounce. Here the bullion value of the 412½ grains silver dollar is $0.849." What is the margin for expenses and profits in exporting a silver dollar to London, exchange being 4.84?

196. What is demonetization?

197. State the causes of the recent change in the relative value of gold and silver.

See authorities under question 202. Crump, 254–267.

198. What have been the great changes in the relative value of gold and silver during the Christian era?

Soetbeer, 114, fg. Chevalier, *Economie Politique*, III., 354–465.

199. Has the ratio 1:15½ for the value of gold to that of silver any historical or scientific prestige over any other ratio? Note that at the end of the 16th century writers on money regarded the relation 1:12 as "normal" or as "given by God and observed by nature."

Soetbeer, 127.

200. The Alternate (or Alternative) or Double Standard consists in a free mint for either gold or silver, the gold and silver dollar (or other unit) having a ratio of weight (fineness being the same) which is fixed by law.

Bimetalism is a project for forming a league of civilized States to carry out an agreement to coin gold and silver at a ratio of 15½ to 1, on the assumption that fluctuations in the value of the metals can in that way be restrained within such limits that there will be a concurrent circulation of the two metals, and that the whole amount of both metals may be available for money.

Expand and explain these definitions. Note especially "free mint" and the function ascribed to law, in the first; also, "project," "league," "15½ : 1," "assumption," "such limits," and the notion about the desirableness of a large supply of money, in the second.

201. Give the history of the French coinage system from 1785 to 1873. Give the history of the Latin Union. Did France resume specie payments in 1878 on the double standard?

Give the history of English coinage since 1700. What brought about the legislation of 1816?

Give the history of coinage in the United States since 1790. What were the motives of the Bland Silver Act? What have been its effects?

Have they been such as the advocates of the act expected? What further effects are to be expected?

Articles on Coinage in Macleod's Dictionary of Political Economy and Lalor's Cyclopedia.

Princeton Review, Nov., 1879, p. 551.

202. The Alternate Standard and Bimetalism or Concurrent Circulation stand on a totally different plane. The former contains no scientific absurdity. The question of adopting it is purely one of expediency. A concurrent circulation is a scientific absurdity and a practical impossibility. It is scientifically as absurd as perpetual motion, or perpetual inertia, because it proposes to annul economic force. It is practically impossible because the league of States would become weaker, not stronger, the more members it embraced.—Expand and prove.

Princeton Review, Nov., 1879. Hertzka, 270–288.

Walker, Pol. Econ., 406–417; Money, 243-271; Money and Trade, 136–196. Horton, 29–36. Seyd., 584–680. Giffen, 197–207; 286–310. Sidgwick, 453–4.

203. "Imagine two reservoirs of water, each subject to independent variations of supply and demand. In the absence of any connecting pipe the level of the water in each reservoir will be subject to its own fluctuations only. But if we open a connection, the water in both will assume a certain mean level, and the effects of any excessive supply or demand will be distributed over the whole area of both reservoirs." Show the fallacy of this analogy to prove that a compensatory action can be established by the mint law fixing a ratio of value of gold to silver, by which compensatory action fluctuations in the value of the metals will be neutralized.

Jevons, Money, 139-40.

204. Supposing that the bimetalic project could be set going, and that the theory on which it is based were sound, and that a new supply of gold should be won from a new California, what would be the effect on the interests of different parties?

Hertzka, 277.

205. Why did the Latin Union close its mints against silver in 1874, and following years? Was the so-called "compensatory action" of the French system accomplished at a loss to France or not?

Hertzka, 268.

206. If it should be granted that the alternative standard favors debtors, and that it is right to favor debtors, would that exhaust the effect of the alternation? If not, what would be its wider effects on classes and nations?

Hertzka, 291-298.

207. Under the alternate standard the standard of value would have more numerous fluctuations, but less wide fluctuations, than under a single standard.—Prove this. Which is the more important fact in regard to fluctuations, magnitude or frequency?

208. Is anyone the richer by obtaining money unless by way of gift, theft, or gambling? (M. 899.)

209. In 1880 the nickel in a five-cent piece was worth three cents. The silver in four quarters or ten dimes was worth eighty cents—"cents" being hundredths of a gold dollar. A, B, and C each paid a five cent fare. A, paid with a nickel five-cent piece. B, gave a trade dollar which was taken for ninety cents. He received three quarters and a dime in return. C, gave a gold dollar and received three quarters and two dimes. What value in gold did each pay for his ride?

210. Herbert Spencer argued that the function of coining money would have been better performed by private enterprise. Jevons objected that the gain in coining comes from making bad money not good, so that competition would run downwards not upwards. Hence, he thought that coining was a peculiar industry which the State ought to, or must, undertake. A third person, commenting on this difference of Spencer and Jevons, said that, if governments had left coining to individual enterprise, the Rothschilds would have given us a universal money fifty years ago.--Who was in the right, and why?

Jevons, Money, 64, 82. Spencer, Social Statics, 438. Cf. Sidgwick, 450–452.

211. Credit is not a thing but a personal relation. Hence it cannot be capital. It transfers capital.—Expand and illustrate this statement, or refute it, if you think it incorrect. Show the advantages of credit and how it aids industry.

212. A bank is an institution which facilitates the borrowing and lending of capital.—Expand and explain this definition. Show what false notions of a bank it excludes. Does a bank deal in credit or debt? Is it an essential function of a "bank" to issue notes?

Sumner, Jackson, 230, 233–4, 319, 362.

213. Balance Sheet of an English Country Bank.

Liabilities.	*£ million.*	*Assets.*	*£ million.*
Deposits, ...	1.74	Cash, in London, and at call,	.27
Circulation, ...	.05	Government funds, . .	.33
Acceptances of London bankers, ...	.01	Indian and colon. gov. secur.,	.44
Capital, ...	.18	Other securities, . .	.06
Guarantee fund, . .	.04	Discounts, . .	.14
Profit to date, . .	.01	Loans, ...	.74
		Bank premises, . .	.03
	2.05		2.05

What does this statement show in regard to the kind and proportion of the operations of this bank, its prosperity, and its ability to withstand a financial storm?

Gilbart, 98–108; 470–488.

214. Balance Sheet of a Scotch Bank.

Liabilities.	*£ million.*	*Assets.*	*£ million.*
Deposits, ...	10.08	Cash on hand or in London,	2.08
Circulation, . . .	.60	Consols and colon. secur.,	1.43
Fourteen day drafts, .	.13	Bk. of Eng. and other stocks,	.38
Acceptances, . .	.17	Discounts, ...	6.85
Capital, ...	1.00	Short loans, . .	1.58
Rest or reserve, . .	.75	Secur. against acceptances,	.17
Semi-ann. dividend, .	.07	Bank premises, . .	.20
Balance, ...	.02	Property paying rent, .	.13
	12.85		12.85

What can you learn from this statement about the kind of business which the bank is carrying on, its prosperity, and its power to stand against a financial storm?

Gilbart, 489–522. Macleod, Dictionary, Banking in Scotland.

215. Balance Sheet of a London Joint Stock Bank.

Liabilities.	*£ million.*	*Assets.*	*£ million.*
Deposits, . . .	23.09	Cash and in Bk. of Eng., .	2.86
Circular notes of, .	.56	Money at call and short notice, . . .	3.71
Acceptances, . . .	.52	Government securities, .	3.57
Endorsements, . .	.07	Indian gov. secur., .	.75
Capital, ...	2.80	Discounts and loans, .	17.15
Rest, ...	1.64	Liability of customers for acceptances, . .	.52
Profits, ...	.25	Liability of customers for endorsements, . .	.07
		Bank premises, . .	.30
	28.95		28.95

Criticise as in question 214.

Gilbart, 462–470. Crump, 23–32.
Bagehot, 243–266.

216. Weekly Statement of the Bank of England.

Issue Department.

	£ million.		*£ million.*
Notes issued, . . .	38.01	Government debt, . .	11.01
		Other securities, .	4.73
		Gold coin and bullion, .	22.26
	38.01		38.01

BANKING DEPARTMENT.

	£ *million.*		£ *million.*
Proprietors' capital, .	14.55	Government securities, .	13.67
Rest, ...	3.09	Other securities, .	20.13
Public deposits, . .	3.51	Notes, ...	11.90
Other deposits, . .	25.02	Gold and silver coin, .	.68
Seven day and other bills,	.22		
	46.40		46.40

The Old Form.

Liabilities.	£ *million.*	*Assets.*	£ *million.*
Circulation, . . .	26.33	Securities, . . .	35.01
Public deposits, . .	3.51	Coin and bullion, .	22.95
Private deposits, . .	25.02		
	54.87		57.96

Balance £ 3.09 mill. as in the Rest above.
Rate of discount, 3 per cent.

Describe from this statement the organization and operation of the bank. How much was the "reserve?" What was the per centage of reserve to cash liabilities? Give the same points as in the last three questions.

Gilbart, 21–71; 254–277. Crump, 268–307. Price, 419–436.
Bagehot, 160–243. Hankey, 73–124.

217. What are the peculiarities in the condition of the bank in each of the following statements?

ISSUE DEPARTMENT.

	£ *mill.*		£ *mill.*
Notes issued, . . .	49.2	Gov. debt, ...	11.0
		Other secur., . .	3.9
		Gold coin and bullion, .	34.2
			49.2

BANKING DEPARTMENT.

	£ mill.		£ mill.
Capital, ...	14.5	Government securities, .	15.2
Rest, ...	3.6	Other securities, . .	16.0
Public deposits, . . .	6.5	Notes, ...	21.4
Other deposits, . . .	28.2	Coin, ...	.8
Seven day and other bills,	.3		
	53.4		53.4

Discount, 2 per cent.

What was the active circulation?

ISSUE DEPARTMENT.

	£ mill.		£ mill.
Notes, ...	33.7	Gov. debt, . . .	11.0
		Other secur., . .	3.9
		Gold coin and bullion, .	18.7
			33.7

BANKING DEPARTMENT.

	£ mill.		£ mill.
Capital.	14.5	Gov. secur., ...	11.7
Rest, ...	3.1	Other secur., . .	20.7
Public deposits, . . .	3.9	Notes, ...	7.4
Other deposits, . . .	18.4	Coin, ...	.6
Seven day and other bills,	.4		
	40.5		40.5

Discount, 9 per cent.

ISSUE DEPARTMENT.

	£ mill.		£ mill.
Notes, ...	21.1	Gov. debt, . . .	11.0
		Other secur., . .	3.0
		Gold coin and bullion, .	6.6
			21.1

BANKING DEPARTMENT.

	£ mill.		£ mill.
Capital, ...	14.5	Gov. secur., ...	9.4
Rest, ...	3.5	Other securities, . .	26.1
Public deposits, . .	5.3	Notes, ...	.9
Other deposits, . .	12.9	Coin, ...	.5
Seven day and other bills,	.8		
	37.0		37.0

Discount, 10 per cent.

218. STATEMENT OF A NATIONAL BANK.

Liabilities.	$ *thousand.*	*Resources.*	$ *thousand.*
Capital, ...	464.	Loans and discounts, .	708.
Surplus, . . .	203.	Over-drafts, . .	.1
Undivided profits, . .	53.	Bonds to secure circulation (par value), . .	450.
Circulation, .	404.	Other stocks and bonds,	163.
Deposits, ...	419.	Due from reserve agents,	105.
Due banks, . .	27.	" " banks, . .	21.
		Banking house, .	32.
		Current expenses and taxes,	3.
		Checks and cash items, .	4.
		Exchanges for Clear. House.	11.
		Notes of other banks, .	15.
		Gold, . . .	30.
		Silver, ...	.9
		Legal tenders, . .	9.
		Redemption fund in U. S. T.,	20.
	$1,574.		$1,574.

Criticise this statement in the same manner as in question 214.

H. A. Richardson, National Banks.

219. "So many convertible bank-notes will the public use as it has a positive need for in paying with bank-notes and no more."—Expand and explain. How does this assertion bear on the question whether "paper is better than specie?"

Price, 418.

220. Criticise the notion of what a banker does which appears in the following: "We have to consider that the banker to a great extent produces the money he lends, viz: his own obligations, which so long as his business flourishes, he is practically never compelled to redeem; and that he may easily afford to sell the use of this commodity at a price materially less than the rate of interest on capital generally." A banker's rate for commercial bills may be less than the rate of interest "since a comparatively low rate of interest on the medium of exchange inexpensively produced by the banker himself would be sufficient to give him normal profit on his banking capital." For "banker" read counterfeiter and so test the notion.

Sidgwick, 262. Price, 444–458.

221. A banker "may be only just able to pay what he owes to others, and yet be, so long as his credit lasts, a wealthy man. Suppose that he owes £1,000,000 (without interest) [deposits. etc.], and has debts of merchants, railway companies and the government, which together could be sold for £1,000,000. If there were a run on the bank and he had to suspend payment, his wealth would be found equivalent to zero; but meanwhile he obtains the interest on £1,000,000, which will leave him a handsome surplus after paying the expenses of the bank. And since there is no reason why he shall not continue to enjoy this surplus for an indefinite period, his business might obviously be sold for a considerable price, even though its assets did not balance its liabilities, provided that the sale were a secret one, so that its credit could be maintained." Would such a man add to the wealth of the country? We formerly had bankers of this description in the United States but we came to regard them as swindlers. Were we wrong?

Sidgwick, 129.

222. Define the "currency principle" and the "banking principle."

Walker, Money, 422–442; Pol. Ec., 178–180.

223. How would you calculate the value to a national bank of its circulation? Suppose that a bank is formed on 4 per cent. bonds which cost

122 and have 20 years to run, the rate of discount being 5 per cent., what is the profit on the circulation?

224. "Explain the remark of an eminent banker: 'If a customer asked me to lend him 10,000 sovereigns, I should answer: Withdraw. If he asked me to lend him 10,000 pounds, I should answer: Let us discuss the matter.'" (M. 1065.)

225. "What would be the effect if all the bank-notes in the Banking Department of the Bank of England were suddenly destroyed?" (M. 1152.)

226. In a period of depression there is just as much currency in the country as ever, but large sums lie in banks, and the rate of discount on call loans is exceedingly low. Why? (M. 1220.)

227. What is the money market? What is dealt in there? What more correct designations might be used?

228. What is the difference between stocks and bonds? What are preferred stocks and second mortgage bonds? What are coupon and registered bonds?

229. It is taught that the rate of interest depends on the supply and demand of capital. In times of crisis excessive rates of interest are paid for the loan of bank notes, even of a suspended bank. Why? and how is such a fact to be reconciled with the doctrine first stated?

Adam Smith, I., 357. Walker, Money, 94–98.

230. Define carefully legal tender, showing what it is and what it is not. Could Congress make bits of colored paper circulate by declaring them "legal tender?"

Princeton Review, November, 1879, p. 561.

231. Which is the better kind of paper currency, a government issue (greenbacks) or an issue guaranteed by the government (national bank notes)? Give reasons in full.

232. If we had no public debt could we have no national banks? or no national currency? If greenbacks should be called in, paid, and burned, and if the national bank note currency should all be surrendered, and if no state banks were allowed to issue notes, what would be the effect on our interests or our convenience, and what should we probably do?

233. Apply the theory of value to inconvertible paper currency issued by a government.

234. Whenever instruments of credit are generally used as the solvents of contracts, and as the things which are passed from hand to hand instead of money, and in order to avoid the use of money, such instruments of credit bear upon their face the word "dollar," "pound," "franc," etc., by which they refer to coined money which has acquired a traditional and habitual, but variable purchasing power. What is the difference between a bullion note, a convertible bank note, and an inconvertible treasury note, in their relation to the coin whose name they bear?

235. The "fiat money" doctrine is that the government stamp gives the value to a coin; that the "dollar" is an ideal unit; and that the government can just as well issue a note bearing the inscription: "This is one dollar by Act of Congress." What effect would it have on this theory if at the same time a new name should be invented for the "ideal unit of value," say, a "Washington," and the note should read: "This is one Washington by Act of Congress?" Could such a note "measure value?" If not, how or why could a greenback do so before 1879?

Walker, Money, 280–290.

236. If the United States should issue "fiat money" now, how would it be brought into circulation?

Walker, Money, 288–289.

237. Can you trace any connection or relation between paper money inflation and the rise of city real estate?

Mann, Chap. X.

238. "A shrinking volume of money transfers property unjustly, and causes a concentration and diminution of wealth. It also impairs the value of existing property by eliminating from it that important element of value conferred upon it by the skill, energy and care of the debtors from which it is wrested."

239. The people of Guernsey wanted a market, but had not money with which to build it. The governor issued paper money, receivable for taxes and dues to the island government, in sufficient amount to pay for the market. In ten years the market earned its cost, which was paid into the treasury in the paper money, which was then burned, "and they got a market for nothing—only the credit of the island."

Cf. Jevons, Money, 204.

240. Describe the Clearing House and define the economic advantages of it.

Jevons, Money, 263–289. Gilbart, Banking, 451–461.

241. Describe the Check Bank.

Jevons, Money, 290–298.
Macleod, Economical Philosophy, II., 510–514.

VIII.

INTERNATIONAL EXCHANGES.

242. "Is there any essential difference between trade between country and country, and trade between county and county, or even between man and man? What is the real nature of trade in all cases?" (M. 1227.)

243. "We may often, by trading with foreigners, obtain their commodities at a smaller expense of labor and capital than they cost to the foreigners themselves." Explain this.

Mill, 348–352.

244. Define comparative cost of production and show its importance to the doctrine of international trade.

Cairnes, Principles, 307–317.

245. Jevons argues that England never could import coal and carry on her industries in competition with those from whom she bought the coal, the cost of transportation being a constant

premium on the transfer of the industry. Do we not see coal brought from Pennsylvania, Maryland and Virginia to New England to be used in industry? How does that fact bear on Jevons' doctrine? What is the correct inference?

Jevons, Coal Question, Chap. XIII.

246. Jevons argues that coal is exported from England as a return cargo and is essential to her commerce on that account. Why so? Suppose that she should use up her coal and try to import Pennsylvania coal, what obstacle to that would be interposed by the same doctrine when viewed from this side?

247. Give a schedule showing the headings of the accounts which enter into the international exchange. Show from this how fallacious must be any inference about the welfare of the country from the preponderance of imports or exports of merchandize and specie.

248. Suppose that the English wheat crop fails and England imports wheat in great quantities from the United States. How would this probably affect the price of bills of exchange on England, and the price of English products in America?

Mill, 370–374.

249. "He hoped that [the three per cent. loan] would be taken entirely by our own people, so that the country would be saved from the annual drain of a large sum which must otherwise go abroad."

250. The English law ordains that 1869 sovereigns shall be cut from 40 troy pounds of gold, $\frac{11}{12}$ fine. The French law ordains that 3100 francs shall be cut from a kilogram of gold $\frac{9}{10}$ fine. The law of the United States prescribes that the dollar unit shall weigh 25.8 grains of gold, $\frac{9}{10}$ fine. What is par of the metals between the United States and each of the others, and between England and France?

Seyd., 285–290, 301, 346.

251. What is the difference between long and short exchange?

Seyd., 427–433.

252. How is it that it is a mere matter of usage whether we say that exchange has risen, or that it has fallen, when we mean that it has turned in favor of importers?

253. Give a history of the suspension of specie payments by France, 1871—1878. Show how the

currency was regulated while inconvertible, and what currency doctrines were established by that experience.

Bonnet, two Essays on the Payment of the Indemnity and the Management of the Currency. Translated. Appleton: 1875. *Journal des Economists*, 15th December, 1874 (Wolowski).

254. Is it a benefit or an injury to the United States that a part of the public debt is held in Europe?

255. We read in the money article, "Posted rates of sterling exchange were 4.82 and 4.84½. Rates for actual business were as follows: Sixty days, 4.81 and 4.81½; demand 4.83¾ @ 4.84; cables, 4.83¾ @ 4.85; commercial bills were 4.79½ @ 4.80."—Explain this statement in detail. The minimum rate of discount at the Bank of England was 3 per cent. Perform the arithmetical calculation to show why the sixty day bills and demand bills differed just as they did.

Goschen, Chap. IV.

256. American securities are sold in London at an arbitrary rating, £1=$5.00. Why is this arbitrary rating adopted? News was received that 1000 shares of stock owned in New York had been sold and paid for in London at 120 per share. Cable transfers were 4.85. Brokerage was ⅛ of one per cent. on the par value. What was the net cash value in New York of the return for the stock?

257. In 1832 silver was the standard of the United States, the silver dollar containing 371.25 grains pure silver. The sovereign contained 113.002 grains pure gold. The ratio of value of gold to silver was 15.625 : 1. The traditional par of exchange was \$4.44=£1. What per cent. was the true par of the metals of this assumed par?

258. Show, in a gold-producing country, what the relations and interaction of new gold supply, prices, relative amount of imports and exports, and rate of exchange would be.

259. Let it be assumed that 5,000 Americans go to Europe for the summer, and spend on an average \$1,000.00 each; that if they did not go to Europe they would spend that amount of money in American watering-places. State the economic effects of this European travel on different classes of the population in Europe and America?

260. "Whenever our gold is shipped to Europe, it is noticed that we are spending more than we are earning, and whenever a country with our boundless and diversified resources finds the balance of trade against it, every sensible man and woman should understand that it means retrenchment or ruin."

261. "One of the virtues of extending the hand of welcome to the Chinese is shown by the fact that to-morrow one thousand of these leeches leave San Francisco for Hong Kong bearing $750,000 which they have made in this country. More than 800 of them have, moreover, been provided with return certificates, which enables them to return and take away more of our money."

262. "In earlier days the leather made [in California] was shipped abroad or to the East, and some portion of it was returned in manufactured forms. The consumer had thus to pay in the price of his purchases the cost of two or more expensive shipments, and of several commissions. It cannot be for his interest to do this, nor for the interest of the cattle raiser, who produces hides, for that of the tanner who prepares them, nor in the broadest sense for the interest of the country."

IX.

ECONOMIC POLICY:

Socialism, Adjustment of Rights, etc.

263. What are the characteristics of an industrial civilization? How does the tone and temper of a people trained under an industrial civilization differ from that of a people trained in a military or police state? Show that socialism is at war with industrial civilization.

Spencer, Sociology, I., 584–590 and fg.

264. In a modern free state, should the question be: Why let alone? or: Why not let alone?

Sumner, What Classes Owe, Chap. VIII.

265. Prove that state regulation of education, factories, food, lodging, etc., is all illusory so long as the state does not regulate family life, or that, if the state is to regulate at all effectively, it must regulate the family.

Letourneau, 401–2.

266. Try to make a formula to define the limits of state interference.

Adam Smith, II., 306. Woolsey, I., 243–269.
Humboldt. Mill on Liberty. Baden-Powell, Chap. I
Spencer, Social Statics, Essays.
Rogers, Art. Free Trade, 9th ed. Encyc. Britannica.
Sumner, What Classes Owe, 112–153.

267. If it could be proved to a laborer that a man of his class in the 13th century had better and surer food and clothes than he, he would not for a moment think of returning to the complete status of the 13th century, just on account of what distinguishes the 19th century from the 13th, viz: personal liberty, independence, and civil rights; but these are the blessings of which free competition is the price.—Criticise this assertion.

Cunningham, 387–410.

268. A certain job being offered for competitive bids, one man bid much below any others, being very anxious to get it, and being willing to employ certain means which other contractors disliked, but by which he could make important savings. When the bids were opened his was rejected because, as he was told, he would ruin himself. His plea that he knew his own business was disregarded.—What light did this case throw on competition and *laissez-faire?*

269. The individual's worst troubles come from the cases where the state *cannot* let him alone, because it adopts lines of policy to which he must conform. E. g.: If the state issues paper money no man can separate himself from those who like paper money, and go his own way on his own judgment. The incidental inconveniences of *laissez-faire* are not to be compared with the positive evils endured by a wise minority forced to yield to a foolish majority.—Expand, prove, and collect other instances. Show that the philosophical basis of *laissez-faire* is in the fact that we cannot tell, before the event, who is wise and who foolish.

270. Roscher says: "There is what we might call a public conscience concerning merit and reward, by which a definite relation of the three branches of income to one another is declared equitable. Every 'fair-minded man' feels satisfied when this relation is realized, and this feeling of satisfaction is one of the principal conditions precedent to the prosperity of production, inasmuch as on it depends the participation of all owners of funds and forces." Does this passage describe facts?

Roscher, II., 166. Walker, Polit. Econ., 281–286.

271. If a man takes an axe and goes into the woods to cut wood, what is a "just" return for his day's labor? Suppose that one man's wood lot is half a mile from home and another's five miles from home, is there any case here under the head of "justice?" Can we say that a man "must" get profits on the capital in the axe and wages for his time? What would be the difference in regard to "just" and "must" if another man owned the wood-lot, provided the axe, and contracted with the first man to go and chop the wood?

272. Each productive laborer puts a share into the combined social productive effort, and each gets some share in the total social satisfaction. The proportion of the effort to the satisfaction is determined by supply and demand, under the existing conditions of the industrial system. There can be no possible conception of a "just" return, or of "justice," in this connection, except the true ratio of effort to satisfaction produced by the free play of supply and demand under existing circumstances. — Criticise this statement. Does "justice" have anything to do with the question whether A and B get as favorable a ratio of satisfaction to effort, one as the other? Suppose that A were an artisan and B a flunkey.

273. Distinguish between the right to get, possess, and enjoy property, and the right to be a property-holder. Which is true and which false? What is the fallacy of any notion of natural rights? Is there any physical or metaphysical good which is gratuitously bestowed on the human race? Show that "equality" never can belong to *being* or *having*, but only to the conditions, chances, and burdens which are created by the state.

De Lavelaye, Preface, and 348–353.
Sumner, What Classes Owe, 13–15; 134–136; 163–169.

274. What classes emigrate from Europe to the United States? What classes emigrate from the United States to Europe? Why are the facts as they are?

275. Do you think that there is a tendency of enlightened opinion toward the establishment of a right in every man born on earth to go to, and live on, any part of the earth where he thinks that the environment will be most favorable for such a man as he is? If not, state what modification you would want to make in that doctrine of right before you would assent to it.

276. If a man owns some land, a horse, and a plow, is there any difference in the meaning of "property" as applied to each of those things? If so, what is it?

277. What are vested rights? What significance have they for the happiness of man and as regards the end for which the state exists? Why do some of the greatest difficulties and dangers of a progressive and liberal state arise from them?

Mill, 134.

278. To pull down those who are superior in wealth, culture, talent, virtue, or education is to act like an army invading a hostile country, which should shoot its own advance guard.—Expand and prove this, or correct and refute it.

279. Can any person be held under obligation to contribute to the struggle for existence of any other person, unless the former be shown to be in some way responsible for the latter's existence?—If so, who? and on what grounds?

Mongredien, Wealth, 233.
Sumner, What Classes Owe.

280. Is there any human being who, in any conceivable circumstances, can rightfully say; "I must live"?

281. It is affirmed that the most efficacious cause of the accumulation of great properties is allowing women to inherit on an equal footing with men. Is that true? If so, what bearing does it have on current discussions about inequality of possessions? Would it be, in other respects, desirable to reverse the tendency of modern times in regard to the property rights of women?

Letourneau, 184, 433–4. De Lavelaye, 217–220.

282. A Connecticut farmer declared that he could not "make any money" because he could not hire any laborers. He said that they all demanded too high wages. A New York merchant declared that he could not "make any money" because his landlord demanded an extravagant rent; the landlord declaring that another tenant was ready to pay the rent demanded. A person who had no capital, but who wanted to carry on business, complained that he could "make no money" because he had to pay such high rates of interest for capital which he borrowed. State the true significance of the facts alleged in each case. What is the correct criticism on these complaints when analyzed and generalized? What should we say of a proposed law to provide one with laborers at wages to suit him, another with a store at rent to suit him, and the third with capital at a rate to suit him?

283. "State what you believe to be the chief economic arguments in favor of the succession of relatives to the property left by deceased persons, instead of its lapse to the state." (M. 238.)

Mill, 135. Letourneau, 440.

284. Distinguish between different kinds of factory acts and state their justification. (M. 1386.)

285. Is there the same justification for industrial schools (teaching trades) as for common schools (giving general culture)? (M. 1390.)

286. Is compulsory school attendance justifiable when tax-payers are forced to provide schools?

287. "These wretched people (in the slums of London) must live somewhere, and it must be near the center, where their work lies. It is notorious that the Artisans' Dwelling Act has, in some respects, made matters worse for them. Large spaces have been cleared of fever-breeding rookeries to make way for the building of decent habitations; but the rents of these are far beyond the means of the abject poor. They are driven to huddle more closely together in the few loath-

some places still left to them, and so Dives makes a richer harvest out of their misery, buying up property condemned as unfit for habitation, and turning it into a gold mine, because the poor must have shelter somewhere, even though it be the shelter of a living tomb. The State must make short work of this iniquitous traffic and secure to the poor the rights of citizenship, the right to live in something better than fever dens, the right to live as something better than the uncleanest of brute beasts. This must be done before the Christian missionary can have much chance with them."

288. Would it be expedient for a State to expend capital in creating a colony and persuading its emigrating citizens to go to that colony, rather than to let them go whithersoever their interest might lead them? Would it be for the interest of either Germany or the United States that German immigrants should take possession of one State of this Union and make it a "German State?"

Roscher, II., 371. Adam Smith, II., 134–225.

289. An argument for government favor to capitalists by *not* placing the interest on government bonds at the lowest market rate:

"If we were dealing with the money-lenders of Europe the question would be entirely different; but we are dealing with our own people; we are dealing with women, with children, with those whose property is in the hands of guardians and trustees; with the farmer who has laid aside temporarily a little money; with the merchant who has a little balance which he desires to invest in a security which shall be not only absolutely safe but which he may convert at any moment without loss. Do we want to stand—if I may use the word—jewing with this class of people to see whether this rate of interest shall be 3½ or 3¼ or 3 per cent.? We must remember that what the government will save by cheapening the rate of interest this class of people of whom I have spoken will to a great extent lose."

290. An American hotel-keeper who failed said that "one of the drawbacks with which hotel-keepers have to contend is the constant increase of rent demanded by our landlords just as soon as they discover we are making a dollar." If the principle of the Irish land act is sound should not the legislature appoint a commission to examine into the truth of the alleged fact, and, if it be found true, should not a court be appointed to assess the "fair rent" of a hotel?

291. On what grounds may railroad land grants be justified?

292. It is objected to patents that they establish property in an idea or device, but that no property in an idea or device should be recognized because two men, or any number of men, can use the same idea or device without interfering with each other, or using it up, but that property in land or chattels is recognized because two men cannot use or enjoy them at the same time. It is also objected that patents are given only for *priority*, not for the invention, and that, within the period of the patent, many persons might independently work out the invention, but are debarred from using it, even for themselves, by the patent law.—Criticise these arguments.

293. "A copyright is a patent under another name and applied to another class of objects, writings instead of inventions."—Is that statement correct? Distinguish thoroughly between copyrights on the one side and patents and tariff monopolies on the other.

Ford, II., 58.

294. Why is transportation a matter of so much greater importance in the United States than in England, France or Germany, and why are transportation questions so much more difficult here?

295. It is said that a railroad pool does away with competition. Why is that not quite correct?

296. What are income bonds? What are collateral trust bonds?

297. The trunk lines, by agreement, charge one cent per bushel for elevator work at New York, Baltimore and Philadelphia. The New York railroad commissioners urged that this charge should be abolished at New York. The representatives of the railroads replied that to do so would put the port of New York at a disadvantage. At other ports steamships lie alongside of the pier on which the elevator is, and there is an elevator charge of one cent per bushel. In New York the ships will not come to the elevator but the grain must be lightered in floating elevators. The roads pay lighterage, three-fourths of a cent per bushel, and charge elevator charge of one cent. If the elevator charge were abolished at one place, it would be at all, and that would leave New York at a disadvantage.

Criticise this allegation and inference.

Report, Hepburn Committee, 22–25, 33–4.

298. What is watering stocks? Specify as many varieties of it as you can think of. Could a house, a newspaper, or a race-horse, be "watered" in the same way? Why do we never hear of it? Why should anyone desire to water stocks?

299. A subscribed three shares in a company at par. He received twelve per cent. dividend and the stock was quoted at 200. The company increased its capital in order to extend its business. It did so by allowing each owner of three shares to subscribe for and get one new share for $100. A sold his "right" for $75. After the increase the stock was quoted at 175. Analyze this operation and show its significance for the rights and interests of the public or of any parties concerned.

300. How would you capitalize a newspaper, a lease, a patent right? A company is formed to build a railroad. They subscribe for first mortgage six per cent. bonds in sufficient amount to build it. When it is done they make a stock capital for it. Why do they adopt this method? Criticise it. What should be or may be the amount of the stock capital? This stock capital is said to be "all water." What is meant by

that and is it true? What, if any, property or valuable thing is behind that stock? What is meant by "capitalizing the road at all which the traffic will bear?" It is said to be a wrong to the public to do that. Why? What do you think about it?

301. It is argued against watering stocks that if a railroad doubles its stock it has to raise its rates for freight and passengers so as to force the public to pay profits on the increased stock.—Criticise that argument, taking note of the two cases, one where the road is a monopoly and the other where it is in full competition with others.

302. A few able and unscrupulous men combined and bought, at a low rate, the stock of a railroad which was well situated but badly managed. They subscribed new capital, put it in good order, paid a dividend, and issued a glowing report. The stock rose to a high figure. They then doubled the stock and also issued bonds on the road for a large amount. They paid large dividends on the watered stock and the half shares were soon as high as the whole ones were before. They then bought up parallel and branch roads at low rates and sold them to the former railroad for its bonds. These and

their stock they then sold. Next they ceased to pay dividends and issued a gloomy report. Thereupon the stock fell and they bought it again.—What had "watering stocks" to do with these transactions? What had issuing annual reports to do with them?

303. A patentee found after a few years that his patent brought him in $5,000 a year. Nine capitalists subscribed $5,000 each to buy of him nine-tenths of his right. The ten then subscribed $5,000 each and formed a joint stock company to develop the patent. It had still ten years to run and they expected that it would earn at least an average of $25,000 per year for those ten years. They put the capital of the company at x dollars, of which each of the ten took one-tenth at the start. What difference did it make to any body what the value of x was? If you were one of the ten, at what value would you want x put, and for what reasons?

304. Write a short essay on the postal telegraph. Consider the possibility that telegrams might be sent at a uniform rate as letters now are.

Jevons, Social Reform.

305. Write a short essay on the purchase of all railroads by the federal government.

306. Write a short essay on the nationalization of the land.

Fawcett, Pol. Econ., 6th ed., Chap. XI. DeLavelaye, 320–1.

307. Write an essay on "National Education," i. e., on the proposition, in various forms, to have the federal government meddle with education.

X.

ECONOMIC POLICY:

Public Finance.

308. In what circumstances is it possible to reduce the interest on the public debt?

Leroy-Beaulieu, II., 365–376.

309. Is it possible to pay off a public debt too rapidly? What is the effect of paying it very rapidly?

Sumner, Jackson, 266–72.

310. What measures the burden to a people of their debt?

Is it right to put the extraordinary expenses of this generation as a burden on the next? On what grounds might an argument be made for so doing?

If a nation is young and growing, what will be the fact with regard to the burden of the debt from decade to decade. How does this fact bear upon the policy of heavy taxation now to pay the debt of the U. S. speedily?

Leroy-Beaulieu, II., 308–311; 360–363.

311. What was the experience of England with a "sinking fund" between 1790 and 1828?

Hamilton, 80–171. Leroy-Beaulieu, II., 306–322.
Accounts and Papers, 710.

312. Has the United States ever had similar experience?

Seybert, 759–774.

313. What is the arrangement about the sinking fund of the federal treasury now? Is the sinking fund of any use or necessity aside from the contract with the bond-holders? Has it any value in fact for them?

W. A. Richardson, 82–85.

314. Show that a sinking fund is not a force in itself, and never can do anything towards the payment of a debt beyond just the amount of saving which is put into it.

315. What was the fallacy of deductions from compound interest which were made the basis of sinking fund doctrines a century ago?

316. How is the reduction of the English debt now accomplished instead of using a sinking fund?

Accounts, etc., 720.

317. What are exchequer bills? What is the theory of their use?

Bagehot, chap. IV.

318. It is argued by very sound and conservative economists on the continent of Europe that it is expedient to connect a drawing of prizes with drawings of the public debt for payment, because fortune and misfortune enter into human life, and constantly affect the managers of capital, so that to offer the small fund holder a chance of a bit of good fortune is only to give him a chance of the same kind.—Criticise this argument.

Leroy-Beaulieu, II., 246–250.

XI.

ECONOMIC POLICY:

Taxation.

319. Define taxation. Show its relations to economic science and statecraft. Show what importance it has for the welfare of the people. Distinguish between arbitrary exactions by irresponsible officials where public peace and security are not assured; taxes laid for other purposes than revenue and having no relation to good government; and strictly economical taxation for which the citizen gets peace, order, and security.

320. The discussion of the canon that taxation should be equal has been much confused by the fact that the disputants sometimes mean equal with respect to units of commodity or property or income, and sometimes equal with respect to the personal circumstances of the different individuals taxed.—Expand and explain this statement.

321. Taxes diffuse themselves on the line of least resistance.—Expand and prove.

322. The parties to an exchange share in all the burdens and hindrances of the same in the direct ratio of their eagerness for the exchange, and they share in the profits and advantages of the same in the inverse ratio of their eagerness for the exchange. This applies to taxes, freights, etc.—Prove this proposition.

Mill, 354–356.

323. From what sources are the revenues of Great Britain obtained now? From what sources are the revenues of the United States obtained? Make a comparison of the two systems of revenue.

Wilson, 109–130. Ford, II., 137–149.

324. Give the history of financial reform in England during the second quarter of this century.

Wilson, 66–85. Mongredien, Free Trade.
Martineau, vols. 2, 3 and 4.
Levi, British Commerce.

325. What are the main points in the Peel-Gladstone system of national finance?

Giffen, Chap. IX.
Molesworth, England, II., 50–228; II., 380,—III., 225.

326. "Under what circumstances are taxes on wages transferred to the employer of labor?" (M. 1555.)

Adam Smith, II., 460–463 ; 466–472. Mill, 498–499.

327. Criticise the Prussian class-tax.

Leroy-Beaulieu, I., 276–280 ; II., 459–461.

328. Discuss the arguments for and against a legacy and succession tax.

Adam Smith, II., 453–4. Mill, 495. Jevons, Coal, 365.
Leroy-Beaulieu, I., 489–500. Letourneau, 440.
Sumner, What Classes Owe, 49–50.

329. Discuss taxes on railroads.

Sidgwick, 574. Leroy-Beaulieu, I., 542–545.

330. Discuss an export duty on raw cotton; on wheat.

Mill, 512–514 ; 515. Sidgwick, 576.

331. How are we interested in the repeal of the Brazilian export duty on coffee?

332. Coal is essential to England's industry. It has been feared that her supply would be exhausted, and it has been proposed to put an export duty on it. Would that be wise?

Jevons, Coal Question, 260–261 ; 276–278 ; 354–360.
Fawcett, Free Trade, 163–4.

333. Write an essay on income tax, including progressive income tax.

Leroy-Beaulieu, I., 126–164; 422–470.

334. Write out the notes of a speech which you would make, if you were a member of Congress this winter, and it was proposed to abolish the duty on sugar.

335. Draw up a budget for the United States for the fiscal year 1883–4 on the basis of the expenditures of 1882–3, showing what taxes or other means of revenue you would employ to provide the required amount.

XII.

ECONOMIC POLICY:

Protectionism.

336. What is the English system of free trade? England levies taxes on some imported commodities. How is this fact to be understood when she claims to have adopted free trade?

Sumner, Protection, 10.

337. Discuss export duties on raw materials and fuel, prohibitions on the export of machinery, prohibitions on the emigration of laborers, bounties on the export of finished products, and taxes on the imports of commodities, in their relations to each other and as parts of a general system.

Adam Smith, II., 79–99; 120–122; 226–246.
Sumner, Protection, 31.

338. Are there are any economic advantages in being the first to take a wise or right course? Does a merchant or manufacturer argue well who says: "I must cheat or I shall be beaten by my rivals who cheat?" Can you illustrate your answer by industrial copartnerships or free trade?

If all men were honest, would honesty have commercial value?

Mongredien, Wealth, 209–212.

339. Mill says (p. 515): "Those are therefore in the right who maintain that taxes on imports are partly paid by foreigners; but they are mistaken when they say it is by the foreign producer." What foreigner is it who pays? and what is Mill's argument?

340. It is said that exigencies arise in the history of a country when it just needs a little help to lift it over a difficulty. Criticise that notion. It is said that a protective tariff is just what is needed to give the assistance. Assume the general notion to be true and criticise the special device here proposed.

Princeton Review, March, 1881, p. 247.

341. State any proposition which you think you can maintain about the relation between high or low wages and international competition.

Sumner, Protection, 22, 42; Argument, etc., 10.

342. In the United States employers say that they need protection because they have to pay high wages. Employees say that they want protection so as to make their wages high. In Germany employees say that they want protection because their wages are low. In each case "high" or "low" is taken with reference to English wages. Criticise these arguments separately and in relation to each other.

Sumner, Argument, etc., 8, 9.

343. If a man goes into a store and finds a piece of cloth such as he wants, does it make any difference to him, in any point of view, whether the cloth was made across the street or across the ocean? What about the cloth alone makes a difference to him?

344. Show the inconsistency between laying heavy duties on commerce and dredging out harbors; between taxing commerce and subsidizing ships; between protecting manufacturing and giving land grants to railroads which make new land accessible.

Sumner, Protection, 14; Jackson, 183–4.

345. Show that, if the protectionists are right in laying taxes "to develop our resources," resources are calamities. Why was the discovery of a nickel deposit in the United States a misfortune, and why may we regret that a tin mine has just been discovered?

346. Show the fallacy of the protectionist argument that capital, which would otherwise be unemployed, is, by protection, drawn into use; that a higher organization of industry is brought about which increases production.

Sumner, Argument, etc., 5.

347. One country has a good and cheap government and therefore low taxes. Another country has a bad and very expensive government, and therefore high taxes. In the first, industry is very free and secure. In the second it is trammelled and uncertain. The former therefore beats the latter even in its own markets. The producers of the latter therefore demand a protective tax to "offset the heavier domestic taxes which they have to pay," and "to put them on an equality with their rivals." After such tax is laid, how many independent evils is the second country suffering from?

348. Show the fallacy: "The money to replace what has been burned [at Chicago] will not be sent abroad to enrich foreign manufacturers, but, thanks to the wise policy of protection which has built up American industry, it will stimulate our own manufacturers, set our mills running faster, and give employment to thousands of idle workmen." Was the fire a calamity?

Compare this case: When Pittsburg was burning in 1877, during a riot, the bystanders refused to put out the fire, saying: "Let her burn, boys! It will make work."

Cairnes, Principles, 253. Sumner, Argument, etc., 8.

349. A process having been discovered for utilizing as fuel great mountains of refuse which has hitherto accumulated at the mouth of coal mines, the production of steel rails is greatly cheapened for the mills which are near the coal mines. The competition of these mills closes up others less favorably situated. Is this course of things a calamity to anybody? If so, to whom? Is it not a misfortune and injustice to the owners and laborers in the mills which are closed that they are not allowed to set up a tariff wall around themselves?—Suppose that the cheapening of production had been accomplished in a foreign country and was not available here, and then answer the same questions.

350. "Upon what a narrow and stupid basis do they discuss this American system of industry! They speak of it as if it were protection of the mill owners, of the mine owners, of the proprietors and managers of furnaces and of railroads and of ships. Why, of course, they have their share in the workings of industry, but the object of it all, and the political reason of it all, is that we mean to protect our wages from being beaten down by the peasantry or the laborers of foreign countries, whose dignity, whose manhood, whose equality is not preserved."

351. "It is not enough to show that iron costs less in England than it costs here. The question is whether iron would not cost far more here, if this country, with its enormous demand, were dependent upon British manufacturers for iron." Discuss the argument that we ought to develop industries at home by protection in order not to be at the mercy of foreign monopolists.

352. "In the first place, I freely grant that the enhanced price of the protected articles represents a loss to the consumers, and through them to the nation. Against this loss I claim that the following gains, where they are gains, should be offset:

First—Any effect that protection may have on the "margin of cultivation."

Second—Any effect upon the equation of international demand.

Third—Any effect upon the employment of classes (women and children) who would not have found employment at all in unprotected industries.

Fourth—Any tendency that engaging in the protected industries may have in employing skilled in the place of common labor.

Fifth—Any tendency which protection may have to lead a nation to save rather than borrow the capital its industries call for.

Sixth—Any influence which protection may have upon the state of the arts and the progress of invention, both in the nation and in the world at large."

Examine these points. Are there such gains? Can protective taxes win them?

353. "We must remember that a worker may gain more by having his industry protected than he will lose by having to pay dearly for what he consumes. A system which raises prices all round—like that in the U. S. at present—is oppressive to consumers, but is most disadvantageous to those who consume without producing anything, and does little, if any, injury to those who produce more than they consume."

354. "Last year, notwithstanding the high duties, we imported of iron and steel, in their various forms, a million and a half tons. These required, for their production, twenty-eight million days' work, and if made in our country would have given steady employment at two dollars a day, to one hundred thousand men, for eleven months, and have left all the profits here, instead of in England."

355. "What I hope I have done is to show that 'capital' is subject to the law of supply and demand. There are many things which affect the rate at which accumulation will go on. Its ultimate amount, however, is always limited, at least as to circulating capital, by the number of laborers, and the average amount of capital that can be profitably utilized in employing them. When accumulations exceed this point one or more of three things may occur: 1. An increase of laborers. 2. Transferring some of them to industries in which it takes more capital per capita to keep laborers at work; or, 3, an accumulation occurs which depresses profits and causes an industrial stagnation.

Now, when protection diverts labor from agriculture to manufacturing it allows accumulation to go on to a point it could not otherwise reach, because it transfers labor to employments requiring more capital.

The yearly profits on such accumulations are a pure gain to the country, and a valid offset against the loss to the consumer, which is the only economic effect free traders seem able to comprehend."

356. Criticise the policy of commercial or reciprocity treaties.

Fawcett, Free Trade, Chap. 6. Baden-Powell, 273–278.

357. The imports of the United States are not sufficient to give return cargos for the ships which are required to take out the exports. Therefore the steamers put in bunks for the westward passage and compete with each other for emigrants. Show how the tariff intensifies this relation of things. What, then, is the effect of the tariff on the net return for American wheat and cotton, on immigration, and therefore on the wages of American wage-receivers?

Cf. Jevons, Coal, 253 fg.

358. Describe the comparative results of free trade and protection in Victoria and New South Wales.

Baden-Powell, Chap. V.

359. The Duc de Broglie wrote a book to prove that under free trade the "less favored nations" would lose population and capital which would find better employment elsewhere. To counteract this he would not adopt the protective system, "nursing father of ignorance, laziness and routine," but would adopt freedom of commerce "under the reservation of the exceptions of which it admits and in the limitations which science sets for it, and with liberty to extend the limitations and exceptions according to national circumstances."—Criticise this proposition. If the whole population and capital of France should move to Greenland, what harm would it do to anybody?

360. "It might shake the Victorian protectionist's faith in his own doctrine if he would reflect that his most effectual protection against the foreigner would be the exhaustion of his own gold fields."—Why? Put American for Victorian, and wheat and cotton fields for gold fields, and say if the argument is equally strong.

Cairnes, Essays, 33–40. Cairnes, Principles, 313–318.

361. If a bounty is paid on exports, who pays it and who gets it?

Adam Smith, II., 79–86. Fawcett, Free Trade, 16–28.

362. "With a perfectly free trade it would probably be impossible for any country to refrain from specializing, while the country that was economically strongest would certainly gain at the expense of others, as it would have an advantage in all the bargains of international trade." Show the fallacy of this passage. Define "economically strongest." Note "all the bargains."
Cunningham, 410.

363. "One land would manufacture and another produce raw materials, so that under a combined regime of perfect free trade no nation would be likely to consist permanently of a mingled population, of whom a large part were engaged in tillage and another large part were in manfacturing." Show, by a study of the distribution and differentiation of industry inside the United States, that this deduction is erroneous.
Cunningham, 410.

364. "A simple case will show how a duty may at once protect the native manufacturer adequately and recoup the country for the expense of protecting him. Suppose that a 5 per cent. duty is imposed on foreign silks, and that, in consequence, after a certain interval, half the silks consumed are the product of native industry, and

that the price of the whole has risen 2½ per cent. It is obvious that, under these circumstances, the other half which comes from abroad, yields the State 5 per cent., while the tax levied from the consumers on the whole is only 2½ per cent., so that the nation, in the aggregate, is at this time losing nothing by protection except the cost of collecting the tax, while a loss equivalent to the whole tax falls on the foreign producers."

Show that the above, if generalized, means as follows: criticise each of the assumptions, and the practicability of the device; note that it is given under the art of political economy:

(1) If a tax of n per cent. is wanted, but (2) if the tax in question may be used up to produce only $\frac{n}{m}$ of revenue, the rest being surrendered to protection, and if another tax may be used for the deficiency, and (3) if the decrease in the total consumption due to advance in price, be left out of account, and (4) if we assume that the price over the whole outside market may be depressed by the tax, and (5) if the loss and waste of years in bringing about the desired result be disregarded, and (6) if the practical impossibility of bringing about the supposed state of things be overlooked, and (7) if the incidence of the tax, variation in price, etc., be measured by the price before the tax was laid, without regard

to deterioration in quality after the tax is laid, then, if a tax of n per cent. causes $\frac{1}{m}$th of the product to be imported and the price to advance $\frac{n}{m}$, the foreigner will pay n per cent. on $\frac{1}{m}$th of the supply and the consumer will pay $\frac{n}{m}$ per cent. on the whole of it, which will be equal. The former will be revenue and the latter can be devoted to protection.

Show that, if all else were sound, this must be modified to read: The foreigner would pay part of the tax, and the domestic consumer might devote to protection a sum equal to that part of the tax which the foreigner pays.

Show the fallacy of the whole argument. If the foreigner lowers his price for the protected market, what is true of the goods which he sends into that market and of his profits on them? Does he really pay any of the tax? Show that the consumer pays revenue n per cent. on $\frac{1}{m}$ imported, and protection n per cent. on the part $m - \frac{1}{m}$ produced at home.

Sidgwick, 491–492.

365. Mr. Ward says that we have now, by our science of sociology, attained to the matter and method of scientific education. Here, then, he thinks, dynamic sociology may begin; *i. e.*, the State may take measures for the application of scientific education and thus move on with regular and uninterrupted steps to the improvement of society.—Criticise this opinion.

366. Show that the improvement of society depends most of all on an advancing standard of parenthood. If, then, we could direct our science of sociology to the object of highest importance, we should endeavor to determine the moral and physical elements of a good parent, and to establish criteria for measuring and defining those elements. If, then, the State were provided by science with these criteria, it would have to determine a standard or limit of good parenthood, and take measures to prevent the marriage of any persons who were below the standard.

Prove the steps of this reasoning. Show why the point of view is erroneous, and why the conception of sociology which is here employed is chimerical.

ESSAYS ON POLITICAL ECONOMY

Excerpted from
Collected Essays in Political and Social Science,
New York: Henry Holt and Company, 1885

William Graham Sumner

CONTENTS.

BIMETALLISM.

IT has been made a ground of reproach against the professional economists that they have not exerted themselves sufficiently to expose the fallacies of bimetallism, but have been contented to pass it by in contempt. Especial point has been given to this reproach by the observation that a great many persons have only resisted bimetallism by a kind of sound instinct. This instinct does not furnish rational ground for conviction, and many such persons have therefore either wavered or been disturbed in their allegiance to sound doctrine. It belongs to the scientific economists, it is said, to show, upon due analysis of the question, wherein the fallacy lies, and to give rational grounds for sound doctrine.

It is not worth while to mention the reasons or the excuses for the neglect to which this complaint refers. If an economist should undertake to expose and combat all the fallacies which gain more or less acceptance, he would not have time for anything else. In the present instance there are more narrow and peculiar difficulties. If one attempts to refute the whole silver doctrine in all its forms, one must demonstrate a sweeping and general negative. If one attempts to select and refute a single form of the error, he will find that no writer on that side of the subject has stated his opinions and doctrines in a form upon which issues can be joined, and a scientific discussion carried on with any prospect of satisfactory results. He will be compelled to argue both sides at once, to put the adversary's case in shape for him before discussing it, and, if he attempts this, he is sure to be entangled in endless charges of misrepresentation and misapprehension. For instance, one writer adopted the term "concurrent circulation," and gave it frequent and current use to express his doctrine and aim. I thought the term well chosen to express the writer's idea as I understood it, and it seemed to me that here was an idea so clear and precise that we could join issue upon it, make an analysis, undertake verification, and so refute or demonstrate, which is what I understand by discussion, and not the heaping together of statistics, historical facts, and authorities. In a later publication, however, the same writer says: "The concurrent use of the two metals, side by side, in the same market is a matter wholly of indifference." We have then this proposition: The bimetallists want a concurrent circulation, but it is matter of indifference whether it be concurrent. There is here, then, no proposition to discuss, but only an illustration of the vague and loose thinking upon which the whole notion of the bimetallists is constructed.[1]

I. What I propose now to treat is bimetallism as it is popularly, however vaguely, believed in in the United States, as it is partially adopted in our legislation, and as it was expressed in the Act under which the Silver Commission was sent to Paris. The appearance of the Report of this Commission[2] furnishes the occasion and the means for examining this notion.

It was provided in the Act known as the Silver Bill that the President should invite the governments of other nations to join in a conference "to adopt a common ratio between gold and silver, for the purpose of establishing internationally the use of bimetallic money, and securing a fixity of the relative value between those metals." The legislators who enacted this assumed and believed that there was no impossibility, in the nature of things, in uniting two metals in the circulation at a fixed ratio of value; they believed that, this plan being debarred by no natural impossibility or absurdity, its expediency could be resolved upon in a conference, and that the means by which it could be realized was an international agreement of the chief commercial nations. I understand that these opinions are held more or less distinctly by all those who are popularly called silver men amongst us. I take issue upon both the points involved.

[1] Mr. Horton uses the term "concurrent circulation" constantly in his essay appended to the Report mentioned below.

[2] Senate Executive Document No. 58, Forty-fifth Congress, Third Session. References to "Report" refer to this document.

1. The first raises a scientific question: Is the notion that two metals can be joined in the coinage at a fixed ratio, by any human device or artifice whatever, true in science? I answer, No; it is just as false as the proposition, A perpetual motion is possible, would be in mechanics. This is certainly the first issue to be settled in regard to the silver controversy as between educated men; but the bimetallists have always slurred it over. At Paris, Count Rusconi did indeed recognize the primary importance of this question in the first session, but much contempt was expressed for the "academic" question, and there was great eagerness to be "practical" and to go on to the "practical" question. This is, indeed, the course of the "practical men," so called. They are impatient of the dogmatism of the professors, who say a perpetual motion is impossible, and insist on going on to consider the great practical advantages which would accrue *if* a perpetual motion were possible, and then, because they think they see such advantages, they go to work to construct the machine. The answer is, that if a perpetual motion, or a bimetallic circulation, were possible, this would not be the same world it is now. It might be a better one, but surely any practical man, in the correct sense of the word, will inquire whether there is any insuperable obstacle, in the nature of things, to the object he wishes to accomplish, before wasting his time upon it. If this is not so, what we call education is a pure waste of time. I had supposed that it was understood and agreed, amongst educated men, that the chief end of studying the sciences was to acquire that training by virtue of which we recognize the relations of man to nature, and the limits of human action.

The inference to be drawn from the importance and true position of the scientific question is not that that question ought to have been discussed in the Conference. Far from it. That was no place for such a discussion. The inference is that the Conference was *ab initio* an absurd and senseless undertaking. The requisite antecedents of any joint action of nations are, (1) that all scientific questions involved shall have been maturely discussed by scientific men until a substantial unanimity of conviction has been reached as to what is true; (2) that these convictions shall have been dogmatically taught in books and periodicals until they have become interwoven with the stock of convictions and faiths of the mass of civilized men; (3) that general opinions as to what it is expedient to do should, by necessary inference, have come to be held by all civilized men. When these conditions are fulfilled it is, of course, found that, for almost all cases, private contract, custom, or the independent legislation of individual states, concurring because proceeding from commonly accepted principles, answers all the purpose. The field for international conventions has therefore hitherto been restricted to postal conventions (common regulations for conducting a form of business which is monopolized by governments, but in which they act like the managers of any other business), or conventions on points of international law (in which the aim is to do justice to humanitarian sentiments wnich have become universal). The difficulty of these latter conventions, even, is instructive for the nature and limits of international conventions, and the history of the Latin Union, as an isolated effort towards international action for other purposes, is certainly a warning and not an encouraging precedent. When, however, the action proposed involves scientific truth, and yet all the necessary conditions precedent are passed over unfulfilled, the proceeding is devoid of sense. It could only have the form of sense if the object were to supersede scientific discussion by action and force—the fallacy of the ecclesiastical councils. The scientific question belongs where I now undertake it: in the forum of academic discussion.

We have then one issue joined; I propose to show that a bimetallic circulation is as absurd and impossible as perpetual motion, so that a convention of the whole human race could not realize it.

2. The second assumption in the Act above quoted relates not to a scientific truth, but to a point of expediency and practicability. It is assumed that an international coinage union, combining and binding the members to a certain programme of action, is a practicable scheme, and needs only a certain degree of consultation to be realized. I shall maintain that such a coinage union is absolutely impracticable. The bearing of this is not directly upon bimetallism, for that is disposed of when it is shown to be absurd, but the coinage union is an element in the

scheme properly known as the alternate or alternative standard. These two schemes, when tested and weighed from the scientific standpoint, are of totally different character and value, as I shall show further on. The question about the alternate standard is a question of expediency and practicability in the main, although it also involves considerations of rights and justice. The difference is that between a perpetual-motion machine and an ordinary machine invented to meet a certain purpose. As to the latter, the questions may be raised whether it will work so as to do what it is made to do, whether it will pay, whether it is dangerous, etc., but if one or all of these questions were decided adversely to the machine, it would still not be an abomination in mechanics like a pretended perpetual motion. The parallel holds in the case before us. The alternate standard is inexpedient for a variety of reasons, and it is impracticable because it involves the necessity of an international coinage union, prescribing regulations and dictating action to its members, and such a union is impracticable. Still the alternate standard involves no scientific absurdity. I therefore join issue, secondly, on the question of the practicability of the coinage union.

II. Before entering upon the subject-matter, a word of explanation is necessary on a certain point. If a monometallist means a man who urges that all nations ought to use gold money, I know of no such person in the world. It is one great error of the bimetallists that they assume to know and judge what money all the world ought to use. No one can reach any such judgment, on the one side or the other, who uses correct processes in the investigation of economic truth. Every nation ought to use just that money which, in its own judgment, its interests and convenience dictate. The economist has to note what course nations pursue under this motive, to study the consequences, interpret the phenomena, and deduce the inferences which are presented to him by the facts themselves. For myself, therefore, I have always repudiated the name Monometallist as a sectarian name, which no scientific economist would be willing to bear.

III. The historical facts bearing on bimetallism and kindred topics have been collected with great zeal during the last few years, but they have rarely been interpreted with the simple fidelity and loyalty just described. Let us recapitulate as briefly as possible, in their chronological order, the facts which are here of importance.

A. The attempt to use two metals together has been kept up from the earliest use of money to the present time, and has constituted a problem in money. It was deemed necessary to use two metals, but no means has ever been devised for using two which has not failed, besides producing confusion, loss, injustice, and commercial distress. In 1717, still essaying to solve the same problem, the English guinea was rated at 21 silver shillings. It was not worth that amount, and so became the cheaper medium, and the standard of prices and credits. The good silver coins were melted, and those which remained were clipped so as to be worth less than $\frac{1}{21}$ of a guinea. After the clipping once began, it went on from worse to worse, as always under the same circumstances, but the need for "change" kept the silver coins afloat. After the middle of the century the depreciation became so great that it led to a clipping of the gold coins also. In 1773 silver coins were made legal tender for no sums over £25, by weight, at 5*s.* 2*d.* per oz. In 1785 France adopted the ratio of 1 to 15½ in a reformation of the coinage, as another attempt to hit the true ratio and keep the two metals in circulation. In 1803 the same ratio was ratified. The French law of 1785–1803 was therefore no new or special solution of the coinage problem, but only another attempt such as those which had been made before. Under the operation of this law, France used silver as a standard until the middle of the century. In 1816 a new coinage system was adopted in England which really accepted and put into a system the state of things which had grown up by custom during the last century—single gold standard, with silver subsidiary depreciated coins, limited in amount, and limited legal tender. It was from a study of the phenomena produced during the previous century by the operation of the laws of trade upon the legal system that the English statesmen were led to this system. The law, therefore, followed custom and the laws of trade, and did not attempt to coerce them. The sovereign now became a money of moneys, *i.e.*, other moneys and currencies were common denominators of value within certain local limits. When a second common denominator was wanted to connect the operations of these local areas with each other, the sovereign met the need. That English money and English commerce thus mutually sustained each other was only an illustration of the principle that good institutions support prosperity and prosperity supports the utility of good institutions. The connection between them is organic, not mechanical. In 1834 the United States passed a new law for a coinage of two metals, but purposely rated the metals so as to get gold. In 1853, having obtained a gold standard by the operation of the law of 1834, they reduced all the silver coins except the dollar to a subsidiary condition, and introduced the English system. In 1853–4, by the fall in gold, France, under the operation of her law, became a gold country. She was burdened with the expense of the change from silver to gold, but this was regarded as a slight price to pay for a change which was opportune to her interests. In 1865 the Latin Union was formed. The nations composing it adopted the French law, and became like France, by the operation of that law, gold countries. In 1867 an International Monetary Conference was held, at which it was proposed to establish, by agreement, what existed in fact—the use of gold as a standard amongst the nations represented. After the formation of the North German Confederation in 1867, an event which to a certain extent met the German aspirations for political unity and national standing, it was felt that one of the greatest obstacles to the realization of the further hopes of commercial and industrial greatness lay in the currency of the country. The standard was silver. The coins were cumbersome. The small coin was, much of it, base billon. The bank-note currency also required reformation. After the war of 1870 and the formation of the empire, all the motives for a currency reform were increased in force, and when such reform was undertaken, all the considerations which had weight dictated that it should be carried through to the adoption of the gold standard. The Scandinavian nations followed the example of Germany. In 1873 the United States codified and simplified their coinage laws according to the existing laws and customs of the country, and according to what would best serve the interests of the country when specie payments should be resumed. They struck the silver dollar from the list of coins which the mint was permitted to coin, on which list it had stood as an idle and unused permission, and brought the United States to the simple gold standard with subsidiary silver. In 1873 silver began to fall by important steps. The operation of the French law would now have taken away gold and given silver to the Latin Union. The movement in this direction, however, was far differently welcomed from the contrary movement of 1853. The Latin Union refused to give up a gold currency and take silver, and undergo the loss of sustaining silver besides. It closed its mints against silver, and the "double standard" ceased to be.

1. Any one now who reviews this series of historical facts, not in order to interpret them by some ulterior design assumed to have existed,[1] but for just what they are, will see that there was no ulterior design, no set purpose, no agreement or combination, but that each nation acted as its own interests dictated, and that the concord of action and general tendency towards the adoption of gold on the part of all the great commercial nations, substantially in the order of their commercial importance, constitutes one of those great historical movements which are not to be criticised or corrected, but which impose upon the student the convictions which he is to adopt.

2. It is plain from a correct statement of the facts that the action of Germany in demonetizing silver was by no means arbitrary. It had the fullest motives and occasion in the state of that nation, and its interest and convenience.[2]

3. The action of the Scandinavian nations was not arbitrary or destitute of motive. The movement towards gold was now so far advanced that the small nations were forced to join it in self-defence. The last to join it would be loaded with the discarded silver, and would have to endure a large part of the total loss upon it. This is only an illustration of the rapid impulse with which such movements finally complete themselves, when the forces have acquired momentum.

4. The action of the United States in 1873 was guided by

[1] Mr. Horton (Report, p. 240). Mr. Horton speaks (p. 745) of the "partisans of gold and persecutors of silver."

[2] The argument of Gen. Walker before the Conference was based upon the assertion that Germany's action was arbitrary. See Report, p. 74.

previous legislation, custom, fact, convenience, and the interests of the country, as they then appeared, and, so far as any evidence has ever been brought forward, by nothing else.

B. We come now to the latest incident in this historical development—a case of action which was indeed arbitrary and destitute of motive. The United States were in currency trouble of their own, serious enough and difficult enough, in itself considered, but they enjoyed, from the suspension of specie payments, one incidental advantage. They had no part or lot in the silver difficulty.[1] They had no stock of silver on which to suffer loss. Their laws were in proper shape to secure resumption on the best system of coinage yet devised. They had time before them. They could wait for developments and take advantage of any state of affairs which might arise, without taking any speculative risks at all. Mr. Horton thinks the United States had a great interest because the demonetization of silver made resumption harder. Resumption on silver would have been easier than resumption on gold, just as resumption would have been easier if the gold dollar had been reduced ten per cent in weight, and not otherwise. In this state of things, then, the United States wilfully plunged into the silver difficulty, and, moreover, came forward to tell those who were in silver difficulty how to get out, and volunteered to lead the way. All the other nations represented at the Conference had an interest in the silver problem, but all refused to act, with the possible exception of Italy. The United States had no interest, but nevertheless took action. As a consequence, this nation now has thirty million dollars of capital invested in silver, which is lying idle and cannot be disposed of without loss. This sum and a large amount in trade dollars have been retained at home as a new element of disorder in our currency, instead of following their natural course to the East. If the advocates of free coinage for silver had had their way, we should also have received thirty or forty millions in silver instead of the same amount in gold received this Fall. Mr. Horton is of opinion that this was a noble ac-

[1] I suppose it is necessary to say that the interest of American silver producers was no interest of the United States. The iron producers were in worse trouble than the silver producers, but no one proposed that the nation should expend capital to "bull" iron.

tion, on the part of the United States on behalf of mankind in general, which has rarely been paralleled. It was, in fact, a piece of national Quixotism which has no parallel in history. The same writer quotes this action as an exception or offset to the uniform tendency of the historical events above cited, but its arbitrary and unfounded character rob it of any force for such a deduction.

IV. It is impossible that I should, within the limits of the present article, review and criticise the points raised at the Conference. Two or three of the chief of them here demand brief attention.

1. The American delegates began by slandering the legislation of their country, and it was left for a foreigner to show (1) that the historical facts about the legislation of 1873 were incorrectly stated by the American delegates, and (2) that the United States are a constitutional country, not ruled by plebiscites, and that we cannot plead ignorance on the part of "the people" against legislation constitutionally adopted. Gen. Walker endeavored to sustain the allegations of his colleague by saying that he, although a professor of political economy, engaged, at the time, in lecturing on money, did not know what was going on. It does not appear that this argument elicited any reply. Perhaps it was thought that its force all lay in the recoil, and some wonder may have been excited whether all American economists would have been obliged to say the same. The fact is that the Act of 1873 so simply enacted the existing law and facts that no one attributed any importance to it.

2. The chief reasons adduced for the action proposed by the United States were vague and undefined terrors of consequences from the historical movement we have described. It was alleged that half the money in the world has been cancelled. This assertion has no foundation in fact. The amount demonetized is just exactly what has been demonetized, viz., the amount of silver held by Germany and the Scandinavian States, and to this there have been important offsets. In the first place, there has been the production of gold since 1873, which, according to Soetbeer's calculations,[1] must have averaged one hundred and

[1] *Edelmetall-Production* (*Petermann's Mittheilungen, Erg. Heft* No. 57, p. 112).

twenty million dollars per annum. In the second place, all the silver five-franc pieces in existence have been added to the stock of "money." Before the fall in silver they were worth more than gold and were merchandise. Since they fell to an equality with gold (below it in value; held equal by limitation[1]), they have been available as money. It would be very difficult to show that, comparing 1879 with 1873, there has been any contraction whatever of the metallic money of Europe and the United States. The expansions and contractions of paper money in Europe and North and South America, within twenty years, have had far greater influence on credit and prices the world over than the changes connected with silver.

3. The fear was also expressed that the adoption of gold would destroy the par of exchange with silver countries, and it was urged that the bimetallic system would furnish a "normal" par. What is the "par" of exchange? Exchange is a ratio between two quantities. How can the ratio between two quantities be "destroyed" so long as the quantities exist? The par of exchange is an entirely imaginary mean-line between fluctuations which are constant, and it has no importance except for the academic explanation of phenomena. We can make a "normal" par any minute; $4.44=£1 is as good a par as any. The sovereign and the dollar may then each of them be gold, silver, or anything else; their values will have a ratio to each other, and may be stated in percentages of $4.44.

V. I proposed, however, to examine the bimetallic notion in its essence, and to proceed with that task it is necessary to consider the relation of legislation to value.[2] For the exposition of the bimetallic fallacy, as well as a number of others which are now widely held and even taught, it is necessary to show that legislation cannot affect value at all. If it could, the text-books of political economy are very faulty in their analysis of value, since no one of them specifies legislation amongst the forces by which value is controlled.

[1] The Bank of France in September charged one tenth of one per cent premium on gold over silver.—*Economist*, Sept. 6, p. 1026.

[2] "Let me dwell upon the fundamental error which suggests the measure which has been proposed. That error is the belief that it appertains to governments to call value into existence." (Mr. Pirmez. Report, p. 121.)

1. The value of a thing is controlled by supply and demand and by nothing else. Supply and demand are natural forces and act under natural laws. By this we mean that supply and demand spring into action from the presence, in certain relations to each other, of certain natural facts. The natural facts, in this case, are (1) a society of men having certain needs, and (2) material goods fit to satisfy those needs. The needs of the men for the goods do not exist because the men so choose, but because they are men. The goods are not supply for the needs because the men so decide, but by virtue of natural qualities. Supply and demand are therefore complementary parts of a force which is natural in the same sense that any physical force is natural. This force must arise when its natural conditions exist; it cannot arise unless they exist; when it arises it acts under natural law—that is, produces a regular succession of phenomena in a determined sequence—and the statement of the law in human language must be made by describing the conditions of equilibrium between the complementary parts, since it is by their equilibrium that the supply performs its function, and the needs receive satisfaction, and the economic force is merged in the vital force of man. The action of man on natural forces is restricted to dividing, combining, and diverting them. He can neither create nor destroy them. The forces may be divided, but the sum of the effects must always be perfectly proportioned to the force, neither less nor more. If any portion of the force is missing in the effect, our task is not complete until we have followed it, ascertained its incidence and effect, and united it to the rest.

2. Gold has its own conditions of supply and demand, and silver has its own conditions of supply and demand, and they are both independent of each other. Those conditions are facts in regard to the actual existence of the metals within the reach of man on the one side, and the increasing, decreasing, or changing needs of the human race, as it lives its life on earth, upon the other. Legislation can affect these conditions in no respect whatever. It cannot increase or decrease the amount of the metals within the reach of man, or his willingness to labor to produce them according to the profit of such production. It cannot make men want what they do not want, or cease to want

what they do want. Economic phenomena are due to economic forces, and one of the first lessons the student has to learn is not to rest from his analysis until he has reduced economic phenomena to economic forces and laws.

One might as well tell a physiologist that his science is false because no man ever existed whose organs were all perfectly normal in their functions, as to contradict an economist because no man ever acted from purely economic motives. Indeed the absurdity is far greater in the latter case, since the economist deals with societies, not individuals; so that not only is the inference unfounded, but the fact alleged is untrue of societies. One might as well object against a physiologist, when he states physiological laws, that moral forces (or, rather, more or less immoral forces, for that is what we mean) affect the bodily functions, as to interpose the objection against economic laws that immoral forces affect economic phenomena. The fact in both cases is undeniable; the inference—that these external interferences alter natural forces and laws, and therefore ought to be taken into account in the statement of scientific principles—is equally unfounded in both. One might as well tell a physiologist that a knife thrust into an organ alters physiological forces and laws, as to tell an economist that legislation controls the laws of value. It is because the physiological laws are not altered that the victim dies. The hygiene, pathology, and therapeutics of society are mixed with its physiology in our text-books, but the scientific distinctions must be maintained intact if we would reason correctly. Value belongs to the physiology of society, legislation almost always to its pathology. Legislation creates the conditions of disease, leads to distorted organs, disordered functions, deceptive phenomena (§ 4 below), and taxes the sagacity and clear-headedness of the student to find again the normal forces in their distorted action; but we have to guard ourselves well against the delusion that it changes forces or laws. To adopt that delusion is to lose perception of the difference between social health and social disease. We are struggling here for the introduction into political economy of universal canons of science which are recognized in all other departments which enjoy authority and are making real progress.

3. One chief cause of the notion amongst us that legislation

can regulate the value of money is, no doubt, the provision in the Constitution of the United States that Congress shall have power so to do. Why was it not also provided, in connection with the cognate power "to fix the standard of weights and measures," that Congress might regulate the length and weight of things? Here is a table. It is so long. How long? Just the quantity of extension in one dimension which it has as a physical fact. If you were here, you would see it. As you are not, I have recourse to ratios to other extensions which you do know. It has the same length as the distance from a man's nose to the end of his middle finger. The Congress of the United States, however, has provided an arbitrary standard of length, now grown familiar by use, and if I write that this table is a yard long, it will be a far more convenient and accurate designation, because it will refer to a more accurate length, equally familiar. If Congress had adopted a standard yard as long as what we now call a foot, that would have become familiar, I should then have written three yards instead of one, and the knowledge conveyed would have been the same. Now how large a Congressional majority would it take to make this table one thousandth of an inch longer or shorter than it actually is? The parallel with the case of money is complete. The Constitution of the United States could not confer powers which nature has never given to mankind. Congress cannot regulate the value of money until it can make a man give for a gold dollar one grain of wheat more than supply and demand force him to give, or yield a gold dollar for one grain less than supply and demand will give him for it. To regulate the value of money is to fix prices, and Congress has never tried that since it has existed. Congress can determine how heavy a piece of metal of a certain fineness shall be the standard of value, just as it determines how long a bar shall be the standard of length; but it cannot regulate the value of a coin any more than it can regulate a physical object to make it longer or shorter than it is.

4. The cases of apparent interference with supply and demand by individuals, combinations, and governments are all cases of monopoly, which is only a special case of supply and demand. An artificial monopoly is possible whenever the supply is capable of comprehension and limitation, and the ma-

nipulation of a monopoly consists in so limiting the supply and adjusting it to the demand as to make the market take some amount at some price. If the monopolist wants to sell more, he must yield on his price. If he wants a higher price, he must be content to sell less. It would be a great mistake, however, to say that a monopolist controls value. It is just because he does not control value that he makes anything. There is still a true point of equilibrium which supply and demand would reach, if free, and it is out of the margin between that point and the point at which the monopolist fixes the market price that his gains, as monopolist, come. There is no other scientific explanation of those gains. A "corner" is a modified case of monopoly, in which the first action is exerted upon the demand. All offered is bought at a price above what any other buyer will pay. This operation, however, is only preliminary to the formation of a monopoly, and a monopoly sale. It would be senseless unless there was a demand foreseen, which would, for some reason, be so strong as to ensure the monopolists a sale at a price above what they pay. What the monopolist does, then, in either case, is to fix the ratio at which the exchange actually takes place at a different ratio from that which value would establish. He thereby transfers other men's goods to himself without giving any equivalent, and it is precisely because value gives us a second point of comparison that we are able to say that the action of the monopolist is unjust and oppressive, and that monopolies are justly odious.

5. The apparent cases of legislative interference with value are cases in point. Subsidiary coins are a case of monopoly, and the problem of their management is to limit the supply to the demand of the community for said coins at their nominal value. Paper money is a case of monopoly. The problem of its value, which has troubled so many writers, is to hold the supply at or below the demand of the community for money to do its business with at par with coin. If the supply of paper dollars is made to exceed the number of gold dollars which the country would need, they will no longer hold a value equal to the value of a gold dollar each. The tariff is a case of monopoly. The protected producers can get the market price plus the tariff, only by selling less than the community would take

at the market price. If they increase the supply, they may run down the price in the home market below the price in the world's market. Hence paper money transfers property from its just possessors to the issuers of the paper, without equivalent, and tariffs transfer property from the unprotected owners to the protected producers without an equivalent. The extent to which this takes place depends on the manipulation of the monopoly; the effect of legislation is limited to the creation of the opportunity for a monopoly.

6. Legal-tender laws, when they are what they ought to be, simply enactments of what is the universal custom and understanding, are rarely if ever called into action at all. It seems to be forgotten that this is their original and only proper character, and whenever such laws are proposed or referred to, laws are always meant which involve some coercion, or distortiom of the terms of a contract. Legal-tender laws of this character do not alter truth, justice, or value. They only transfer property. A legal-tender law does not make 90 paid = 100 due a true equation. The only true equation is 90 paid + 10 retained = 100 due. Legal-tender laws alter the line between mine and thine so that something which was on one side is now on the other, but they do not affect the validity of the venerable distinction. The legal-tender law simply provides that the courts which administer justice under the Constitution and laws of the country in question shall not listen, in certain cases, to the plea of the citizen who complains of injustice; in other words, it withdraws the protection of the courts of justice, in certain cases, from citizens who complain of injustice. Some decisions even seem to go so far as to interpret the law so that A may demand B's property and discharge B's claim with an arbitrary allowance to which B never consented. In all cases it is because the forces of nature act in perfect fidelity to their laws that we can see and define the injustice of this legislation. It is because the legislation has not affected the law of value that we can have another state of things in mind as right and just, and can often measure the degree to which legislation has transferred the products of one man's labor and economy to another man's use and enjoyment. It would be difficult indeed to prove that the value of a man's property or his right to it

was affected by stealing it from him. Value is one form of truth, and truth is not affected by majorities. The notion that legislation affects value must therefore be positively condemned as the root-error of a dozen mischievous fallacies. Legislation transfers property, and that is all it ever does.

7. It is necessary to notice also the law which governs all combinations. If a single individual undertakes, for instance, to establish a corner, he may be reasonably sure of his own will, intention, and plan, and may carry it out if he does not lose his head and prove inconsistent with himself—which indeed sometimes occurs. If he finds it necessary to associate another with himself, there arises the need of selecting a congenial comrade and of securing consent, co-operation, loyalty, and good faith between two separate wills. The difficulty of such combination is not double that of an individual operation; it may be twenty-fold greater. If three, five, ten, twenty persons must be combined, the difficulty advances in a tremendous ratio until it becomes a practical impossibility. Hence the manipulation of a corner or a monopoly does not gain force or become easier as the task is widened and the number of participants is increased, but the force decreases in an enormous ratio to the extension of the party, and the practical chances of success diminish in an equally rapid ratio to the number of participants.

VI. Having elucidated these points, which, by the way, show the need, in economic discussions, of firm grasp of elementary notions and principles, we may, in a brief space, bring them to bear on the thesis with which we started.

1. Inasmuch as gold and silver have independent conditions of supply and demand in natural facts, their relative value may remain the same through a long period, or one or the other may grow dearer, and the fluctuations may be rare or frequent, wide or narrow, sudden or gradual, in all possible combinations and sequences. It has been proposed to form an international union, to establish a fixed ratio for the mints of all members of the union, and to make either metal legal tender. By this plan it is proposed to change from one metal to the other as fluctuations take place, and it is expected that the fluctuations will be limited in their range, but it is not expected that a concurrent circulation will be produced, or that the whole

stock of both metals will be brought to act on credit and prices. Reserving for the present the question of the practicability of the coinage union, it may be admitted that, under some circumstances, the fluctuations would be limited, but they would be more frequent and sudden, and the system would be at the sport of chance, as the Latin Union was. These, however, are minor difficulties. The legal-tender law, by which all this is to be accomplished, would simply, as above shown, transfer property. The gain, if any, would be a gain to some at the expense of others. In plain language, the project is one for uniting the debtor classes of all civilized nations in a "corner" on the falling metal. Such a project has no parallel save in some of the wildest plans of the International Society. The profits of the corner would come out of the creditor class and the holders of the rising metal. It would be establishing on a world-wide scale, and by force of law, an injustice by which some men would throw the risks and loss of their business on other men, who already have the risks and losses of their own business to carry. For instance, some Liverpool merchants interested in the South American and East Indian trade have suffered loss by the fall in silver. They are eager for the "double standard" to save them from their losses, and no doubt it would do so, but only by throwing those losses on the whole creditor class of England. Now, the creditor class of England is scattered, unorganized, and unknown, but it is safe to say that it has its own troubles from business and investments, and is suffering from loss of dividends, failure of banks, fall in prices, fall in rents, fire, shipwreck, and all the other chances and accidents of life. The advocates of the "alternate standard" have contented themselves with dilating upon the effect of their scheme in narrowing the fluctuations of the market rate of the metals, without reflecting that no such effect could be attained without an expenditure of force, at somebody's expense, elsewhere.

2. But the coinage union is a practical impossibility. France, a country with a free mint for both metals, standing between Germany, a silver country, and England, a gold country, was able to work a compensatory action between them. There is an obvious fallacy, however, in reasoning that the same action would go on, on a larger scale and with greater efficiency, if the differ-

entiation upon which the interaction depended were obliterated in a coinage union having a uniform system.

There is a further fallacy, and a far more serious one from a scientific point of view, in supposing that the coinage union, if extended, would gain proportionate increments of force to restrain fluctuations until they were reduced to a minimum or to nothing. The law above stated here comes into operation, by virtue of which a combination becomes not stronger, but weaker, as it is extended, and the attempt of all nations to form a corner upon the falling metal would dissipate itself like a corner which united all the buyers—that is, it would become simply identical with demand as we ordinarily use the term. Instead, therefore, of marching towards a realization of bimetallism or a concurrent circulation, the coinage union would work towards the simple free play of natural forces, in which each metal would obey its own conditions of supply and demand. Nor is this all. The coinage union is either unnecessary, or else it is needed in order to impose a set line of action and to enforce co-operation where voluntary co-operation would not be given. How can any one believe that sovereign nations will enter into any such combination, or that, if they did enter into it, they would stay in and obey mandates which conflicted with their interest and will? We are not left to speculation as to the probability that they would so act. We have two facts to which to refer: (1) When the fall in silver took place, the Latin Union would have been disrupted by the secession of Belgium and Switzerland if the coinage of silver had not been suspended. (2) The commissioners of the Latin Union, at their last meeting, agreed that Italy should withdraw her small notes to make room for the return of her small coin with which the other states, especially France, were burdened. I do not understand that Italy has refused to do this, but the remonstrances which were made in the Italian Parliament against this dictation as to what Italy should do with her own currency were just what must be expected in such a case, and they show that an international coinage union would prove a rope of sand so soon as the attempt was made to make it efficient at all. An international coinage union, therefore, to accomplish a definite and set purpose in turning back a movement which all recognize, whether they deplore it or not, is an absolutely impracticable scheme.

3. I have never seen any argument for the feasibility of bimetallism, or a concurrent circulation, in which the whole of both metals would act on prices and credit, except the facile inference that the coinage union as it grew larger would or might restrain fluctuations more and more, to a minimum or to nothing. As I have broken down every assumption here involved, the inference falls to the ground. It appears that this reasoning follows neither a true relation of facts nor any logical sequence. The coinage union as it grew larger and larger would grow less and less effective, and when it was complete it would have no effect at all. The notion of a concurrent circulation is therefore entirely baseless—snatched from the air. So long as the natural conditions of supply and demand of gold and silver remained the same, whether for a longer or shorter period, so long the forces would remain the same, and the effects would remain the same. So soon, whether sooner or later, as the conditions varied, the forces would vary, and the proportionate effects would vary. To secure a concurrent circulation, then, at a fixed ratio, it is necessary to suppress the effects, which can only be done by suppressing the forces, so that a concurrent circulation could never be realized until we could extinguish economic forces by human agency. But we can no more extinguish a force than we can create one, so that this scheme is in economics what perpetual motion is in mechanics. Every analysis that is attempted of the idea will only issue in new proof that it is an absurdity which cannot be thought, and it is no longer strange that its advocates have never been able to state their notion in intelligible language. It must remain vague, shadowy, and popular, stated at best in symbols, metaphors, and analogies, to exist at all.[1]

VII. If the amount of space which would be required were not out of all proportion to the results for our purpose, I should

[1] "As for the desire which has been expressed that the hope be left open that some day a fixed relation may be established between gold and silver and an international value given to them, the English delegate (Mr. Goschen) declared that, in his view, it was impossible to realize this, impossible to maintain it in theory, and that it was contrary to the principles of science." (Report, p. 166.)

like to analyze some of the analogies which have been employed in this discussion. Some of them deserve to be put into the text-books on logic as classical examples of the mischief of reasoning by analogy. An analogy proves nothing whatever. It only serves to state a theorem in a form to be more easily apprehended. The theorem, then, needs to be proven by its appropriate demonstration. After showing the mischievous character of the notions imported into this discussion by the analogies of tubs of water joined by a tube, and horses driven in span, I should not have advanced the discussion in which I am engaged. The bimetallist says: A concurrent circulation seems to me like driving two horses in span. I answer: To me it seems like yoking the sun and moon together to facilitate the reckoning of time by men by making the lunar month a simple fraction of the solar year. Nothing is accomplished by these statements towards testing the truth of either opinion. I therefore pass by all the analogies which have been offered by the bimetallists with the simple remark that they are all untrue and misleading.

The advocates of the goloid dollar, who think they can give greater fixity to the ratio of the metals by mixing them in the same coin, advocate a more grotesque absurdity, but not a greater one, than the other advocates of a "concurrent circulation."

VIII. We must infer, then, that gold and silver will both be used as components in the world's money, by the adoption by some nations of one and by other nations of the other, as their convenience and interest dictate. The United States, by its legislation so far, has put itself on the way to become one of the silver countries. It is not a dogmatic judgment; it is inference from observation of the course adopted by nations, that gold is more convenient for the purpose of the leading commercial nations, and silver for those which are yet behind.[1] The United States is one of those whose interests require the use of gold, and the way back over the path we are now treading will have to be won by trouble, loss, and inconvenience. Our children, instead of admiring our Quixotic devotion to mankind

[1] Feer-Herzog. Report, p. 60.

in general, will ask us how we could ever commit the folly of plunging into a difficulty which everybody else was trying to escape, and from which our children will have to extricate themselves at heavy expense. I am far from denying that the change from silver to gold is attended by loss and inconvenience, but I do not know of any step of social or economic advance which has ever been made without temporary loss and inconvenience both to capital and labor, and the United States were not exposed to any of this loss at all. Mr. Seyd has just published a book, "The Decline of Prosperity, and its Insidious Cause," in which, as the title indicates, he takes a very lugubrious view of things, and ascribes the mischief to the demonetization of silver. This fear that prosperity was declining has come up every fifteen or twenty years for a century or two, especially in England, and yet prosperity and civilization advance. In 1872 coal and meat were dear, and the newspapers were filled with essays about the sufferings of the people on fixed incomes. Then the woes of the agricultural laborers came up, and the farmers were represented as selfish men, gorged with wealth and prosperity. Now meat is too cheap, the turn has come to the landowners, and the farmers are the objects of public concern. Such changes are the inevitable effects of the continual changes in the conditions of industry and the relations of commerce. It is from and by means of such changes that the prosperity of mankind advances. Every great improvement involves changes and readjustments. They are not welcome, but they are unavoidable. It is not at all improbable that the number and variety of the great improvements of the last twenty years, following so rapidly on each other, crossing and combining with each other, necessitating quick and complicated adjustments, may go for a great deal in the present reaction. It is very probable that the next twenty-five years are to see massive migrations of population, and great transfers of capital, from the old to the new countries, which will not be made until suffering has enforced them. It is probable that the value and rent of land will decline in the old countries and rise in the new. It is possible that social, economic, and political changes are to be accomplished such as we cannot yet guess at. It is certain to my mind, however, that those years are to be years of unprecedented prosperity.

The fall in silver has its share in the temporary disorder, loss, and suffering; but the use of the single gold standard will be one of the strongest supports of the new prosperity. If this were not so, it would be idle to lament over a movement which comes along in the natural evolution of things. To try to stem that movement and turn it back to the old system of repeated empirical struggles for a bimetallic circulation, it would be necessary for us to be sure of three things: (1) that we understand present phenomena thoroughly,[1] (2) that we can foresee the results of the movement towards gold, if it goes on, and (3) that we are sure of the working of the gigantic experiment involved in the attempt to secure bimetallism, or the alternate standard, by a coinage union. These conditions are absolutely unfulfilled. On the contrary, it seems that international banking is just at the point where its further development, and the transfer of capital from old to new countries, above alluded to, require an international standard of value amongst the great commercial nations such as gold alone can supply. The development of international banking, in its turn, will economize the use of gold, and thus again defeat the fears of those who think there is not gold enough. The movement, therefore, bears all the marks of a true organic development, in which all the parts contribute to and support each other in advancement to a higher stage. It also seems to me that the fall in silver is precisely adapted to favor those extensions of commerce and civilization which lie in the near future. South America is still in the lowest stage of economic development, and will find silver its best money for a long time to come. Asia is scarcely yet upon a monetary system, except where Europeans have penetrated, and can use nothing but silver to advantage for an indefinite future. Africa is an almost untouched continent, which, within fifty years, will probably come into new

[1] The authorities are by no means agreed as to the causes of the fall of silver. This question came up at Paris, and Mr. Feer-Herzog maintained that the key to the phenomenon lay in the state of the East Indian exchanges. (Report, p. 58.) This is the view which I took before the U. S. Silver Committee in 1876, but I have never seen any other confirmation of it.

relations to the civilized world. Silver is the only suitable medium for this extension of commerce. As far, then, as we can foresee, the cheapening of the tool of exchange by which these extensions of trade and civilization must be carried on will only facilitate them; and if bimetallism were not an absurdity, and the alternate standard either an injustice or a delusion, and if either of them were practicable, the adoption of either would now be the grandest mistake the civilized world could commit. I attribute no weight to these prognostications of mine. It is contrary to my opinion of sound procedure in such matters to make them at all. I should consider it the most vicious procedure to make such prognostications the basis of argument that any nation or that all civilized nations "ought" to use the single gold standard. The economic development of human society must go on its way and work out its results, and the human race must make the best of them. The race, however, does not make mistakes, and so long as, in all its parts, it obeys the dictates of its interests, it will push on a true evolution which cannot but serve to enhance the prosperity of the race as a whole. It is only when nations allow their action to be dictated by speculations about the future of civilization and humanity that they may wreck the natural development. It is because these terrors about the future, and prophecies of disaster, have been introduced to play so great a *rôle* on the other side of this question that I venture to set against them the best speculations I can make as to the probable course of affairs.

POSTSCRIPT.—After the above was in type my attention was called, by an editorial in the New York *Tribune*, to a recantation by Mr. Gibbs of the opinions maintained by him at the Conference at Paris. The plan of my article was to make an independent discussion, and not to examine the literature of bimetallism beyond the Report of the Monetary Commission. When, however, a journal which has sustained a uniformly sound and strong position on monetary questions referred to Mr. Gibbs' pamphlet in the terms used by the *Tribune*, it seemed that here perhaps a bimetallist might at last be found who had some clear ideas, and could state them so as to bear examination. I therefore hastened to secure a copy of Mr. Gibbs' pamphlet,[1] and also a copy of his letter to Cernuschi announcing his conversion, and Cernuschi's reply to the same.[2] My hopes of finding something in these pamphlets solid enough to bear examination for purposes of discussion are all disappointed.

Mr. Gibbs has simply gone over to the bimetallic fallacy, and accepted it in its grossest and crudest form. He has produced no new arguments for it and refuted no objections against it. Incidentally he has shown that the ex-Governor of the Bank of England holds, in regard to money, all the fallacies which constitute the premises of our soft-money men; and if he does not agree with them in their conclusions, it is only because he is less logical and consistent. This, however, might be said of all bimetallists. The *Tribune's* estimate of this pamphlet adds the greatest possible weight to the motive for my article as stated in the first paragraph thereof. I am therefore led to counteract that estimate by amplifying one or two points which I had passed over briefly, and by inserting one or two which I had judged better to omit, in order to show the real significance and value of what Mr. Gibbs has contributed to this controversy.

1. Mr. Gibbs' conversion to bimetallism is due to observation of the losses incurred in Indian finances and Indian trade. He assumes that these losses are due to the fall in silver, and he attributes the fall in silver to demonetization. Hence he argues: Remonetize; that will restore silver; that will stop the losses. It is a pity that the matter is not so simple. I consider it an error to attribute the losses in the India trade to the fall in silver. The fall in silver is not a cause, but a consequence. The financial relations between England and India after 1870 took such shape that the "tribute," as it is called, had to be paid by an excess of exports over imports of India. This could only be accomplished by a fall in prices in India. Nevertheless Europe desired to continue to sell silver to India, while the relation just mentioned would have led

[1] "Silver and Gold," by Henry H. Gibbs, London, 1879.

[2] "Bimetallism in England and Abroad," by Henri Cernuschi, London, 1879.

India to desist from buying it. Instead of a *fall* in prices (silver remaining stable) there therefore has occurred the exactly equivalent phenomenon of a fall in silver *without any rise* in prices. In countries which have a depreciated paper currency prices rise as the medium falls, and so the foreign trade quickly adjusts itself. If prices had risen in India there would have been no trouble; but the forces which would have forced a fall in prices if silver had held firm have prevented a rise in prices while forcing a fall in the medium. A crisis in the Indian exchanges was therefore inevitable in some form or other. Instead of taking place through prices, it has taken place through the medium—silver—and the fall in silver is a consequence and not a cause. This relation of facts accounts for the fall in silver, and nothing else does. The silver thrown on the market by demonetization and by a somewhat increased production (which has been greatly exaggerated) by no means account for the fall. The increased supply fell on a weak market, and had accessory influence, but it does not suffice to account for the principal effect. It follows that it is a great error for those who suffer from losses in the India trade to ascribe their troubles to the fall in silver, and that their troubles cannot be cured by any currency devices. While India has so much interest to pay in England on borrowed capital, to which she has not yet grown up, and while she has to pay in England for an expensive government, to which also she has not yet grown up, she will be a worse country to sell in and a better one to buy in than formerly. However, if English merchants and bankers interested in the India trade could sell their silver to somebody for the old price, it is obvious that they could save themselves from the effect of these changed circumstances in the relations of the two countries.

2. This last observation leads me to amplify what I have said under VI., I. I have shown there that the alternate standard would only transfer risks and losses from those to whom they belong to somebody else. *A fortiori* bimetallism, if it were practicable, would throw all risks and losses, all the time, on the creditor classes. Gibbs and Cernuschi seem to be entirely blind to this character in their propositions, and they do not see that whatever they gain for some must either be won out of others

or *out of nothing*, as I have shown in my main argument. To show this more fully, let us observe the difference for different classes between the significance of a fall in gold and the significance of a fall in silver. The effect of a fall in gold (rise in prices) would fall on annuitants, pensioners, owners of bonds, etc., beneficiaries of trusts and life assurances, salaried and professional men, wage-receivers, and, generally, on all who have either temporarily or permanently fixed incomes. These are the persons whom I designate as the creditor classes. A fall in silver, as things stood in 1873, affected producers, exchangers, and bankers in certain great lines of business. A fall in gold would therefore affect a large number of small, weak, and scattered recipients of money incomes, belonging to different classes and having no co-operation or even acquaintance with each other. A fall in silver affects great "interests," each of which is marked by very strong cohesion of its parts within itself, and all of which are capable of sudden and easy combination. The former have little power or chance to defend themselves; the latter are powerful and influential in speech, writing, and legislation. The former never attract public attention; the latter fill the public eye and are thought of whenever money, capital, trade, or industry are thought of. The losses of the latter make up appalling figures in the statistics of bankruptcy. The losses of the former figure in no statistics, since they consist in privation, misery, disease, and earlier death for those affected directly and for their dependants. The losses to producers, exchangers, and bankers are what govern the opinions of Mr. Seyd, and now, too, have converted Mr. Gibbs. It is indeed cause for great regret that such losses should occur, and if there were any means of averting the loss altogether, the matter would bear a very different aspect. But there is no such means. There is nothing possible but an alternative, either to leave the losses where they fall by the circumstances of the case, or to throw them on somebody else; and nothing is proposed in these monetary schemes save to throw the losses on those who would have suffered if the fall had been in gold instead of in silver. Now when gold has fallen (prices have risen), notably in 1870–1873, the classes who were affected had to make the best of it without aid from those interested in silver, and so the proposition that

England shall now adopt bimetallism, when stripped of all disguises, is simply another case of the old abuse whereby a few strong, well-organized interests, acting through currency legislation, play at "heads I win, tails you lose" with the large, scattered, unorganized mass of the nation. English statesmen may possibly upset the monetary basis on which all relations of property and credit in England rest, in order to alleviate a temporary strain on some branches of foreign trade, and on the finances of India; but those who have to rely on American newspapers for their information and impressions of what is likely to be done in this matter in Europe will do well to nourish an active incredulousness. Those Americans who have to rely on the Hon. W. D. Kelly's reports of interviews between himself and Bismarck for judgments as to the probable course of Germany will do well to allow for other elements in the report than the probable power of Mr. Kelly to inspire the Prince with expansive and familiar confidence. Mr. Kelly is a man of enthusiastic imagination, and it appears probable that he and Mr. George Walker are just the kind of men to excite the well-known propensity of the German Chancellor to befool people by an ostentatious and effusive frankness while laughing at them in his sleeve. A great deal has been said about the zeal, dogmatism, and fanaticism of the advocates of the single universal gold standard. I do not know who these persons are, nor what they have done. The only persons who, in regard to this monetary question, have organized a sect, adopted a creed, undertaken a propaganda, and sent out missionaries, so far as I know, are the bimetallists. It is charitable to believe that they do not see the political and social significance of their propositions, but that statesmen will not see this long before action is adopted is very improbable.

Now Mr. Gibbs has just found out that the trade between India and England is barter. He is astonished and alarmed at this. He thinks this kind of trade uncivilized and attended by loss to England. He attributes the evil to English gold monometallism, and thinks that the evil effects have been counteracted until recent years by the French law. If it be true, however, as Mr. Gibbs and the other bimetallists argue, that France has done this service by her law, now to gold-using Englishmen and now to silver-using Germans, then France, through her creditor class, has borne burdens and losses which belonged to other people. Such being the case, we could see why Englishmen and Germans should want the French law to continue, but we should also see why Frenchmen, so soon as they understood it, would certainly want it to stop; and, if universal bimetallism could be or should be established, the next question would be, What class, under the new system, is to take the place formerly filled by the French creditor class and bear the burdens formerly borne by them?

Such is the inference from Mr. Gibbs' premisses, but the premisses are false. Trade with India is barter, but so is all trade, and foreign trade most plainly. The trade for silver has involved inconveniences which will exist until all the world uses a single and universal standard of value. This inconvenience has been paid for, as all other hindrances and difficulties of trade are paid for, in prices. The French mint law has had nothing to do with it. Finally, the French creditors have lost whenever the ratio of the metals has varied so as to change the metal of the French coinage. This loss, however, has been borne once for all; it has not continued after prices have been readjusted; and has not therefore been constant under the operation of the double standard.

Cernuschi, in his reply to Gibbs, gives far more gross expression to the same fallacy about the operation of the French law to prevent losses; for he attaches it not to English traders, but to all metal producers. "At the time of the French 15½, the position of the producers of gold and silver was this: all their produce had by law an unfailing and insatiable customer —the *mint*. No price to haggle about, no competition possible." A customer by law! The mint a customer!? In some large establishments, as a check on salesmen, one person is stationed at a counter to weigh, measure, and count all goods for which the salesmen have made bargains with the customers. It would be as sensible to call this person the "unfailing and insatiable customer" for all the goods sold in the establishment as to call the mint a customer for gold and silver. This gross error, however, is the cloak which covers the fallacy and the injustice of bimetallism. The law does provide a customer, but it is not the mint. It is the creditor class as above defined. There is "no price to haggle about and no competition to fear" because the law has delivered the victim over helpless, all the more helpless because he is ignorant, the law having concealed the transaction under mysteries of coinage and money. This, however, is the most direct condemnation of the law itself, as well in an economic as a social or political point of view. It is a fallacy to think the mint law has secured the producers of the metals against loss and haggling and competition—that is, against all the inevitable annoyances of industry without hurting anybody else; and it is an injustice to take the annoyances from one industry only to spread them over others. I do not like to say anything which may appear arrogant and unbecoming, but I feel justified in protesting, in the name of all that scholars and scientific men respect, that a man who calls the mint an "unfailing and insatiable customer" does not deserve respectful treatment in the arena of scientific discussion.

Mr. Gibbs sees that bimetallism involves depreciation, but he thinks the evils of it are in this case more nominal than real. The only distinction which men generally make between nominal evils and real evils is that my evils are real and yours are nominal; but that is not a valid distinction which science or justice can recognize. Mr. Gibbs seems to think the evils of depreciation nominal because they would be widely scattered and much concealed, as I have shown above. All evils, however, are real to those who suffer them. If they come from nature, like blight, drought, storms, inundations, and other calamities, they must be borne as philosophically as possible. If they are inflicted by legislation, or are transferred by legislation, nothing can justify or belittle them. Mr. Gibbs wants silver remonetized, not at its present market value, but at the point where it will be when the bimetallic system shall have operated on it. He has not comprehended the full problem which he has to solve. It is this: (1) If in England, for instance, silver is rated at its present market value, all the silver now in England loses 20 per cent of its present value. (2) If silver is rated at the point to which the bimetallic system will bring it up, no one but Cernuschi knows where that will be. If a guess is made, and silver is rated above the market, no debtor will want it, and so the bimetallic system will never begin. (3) If silver is rated at the market to begin with, and if the mint ratio is advanced as the market ratio advances (assuming that bimetallism would work), then continual recoinage, with heavy expense and endless confusion, will result. I hope that it is plain, then, that the bimetallists of every grade and description are either trying to transfer losses from one group of men to another, or else trying to make something out of nothing.

3. It also seems desirable to notice another error of bimetallism which I had passed over; that is the notion that demand due to a fall in price raises price. This doctrine is essential to the bimetallic theory, and it has been carelessly conceded by some who are not bimetallists. I passed over it in the body of my article because it is the fallacy of that extreme form of bimetallism in which it is believed that the coinage union will lock the two metals so tight together that they will never separate from the legal ratio any more, because there will be no one to whom to sell the rising metal. Every bimetallist would be driven to this doctrine if he followed out his notions consistently; but the bimetallists repudiate it generally when it is ascribed to them. Mr. Gibbs, however, explicitly accepts this notion, and assumes that the bimetallic union would lock the two metals permanently together as such an undoubted fact that it is his chief reliance for refuting objections. Demand due to a fall in price tends to sustain price at the lower level, but not to raise price, since such demand ceases when the price rises. If we have a bimetallic circulation at 15½ to 1, debtors do not want silver *at* or below 15½ to 1, but only below. Their demand will only act on it so long as it stays below; therefore their demand never can lift it again to 15½ to 1. But meanwhile their demand is acting to sustain it only by absorbing any new supply through real purchases. So long, therefore, as there is a new supply, the price must remain below 15½ to 1, and that new supply must be absorbed. But this is destroying the bimetallic and concurrent circulation just so far as it goes on. The bimetallists seem to think that, *if* silver fell, the debtors of the world would all pounce upon it so unanimously and immediately that it would *not* fall. This is absurd in the statement, and it is absurd in every detail of fact. New silver does not rain down in an equal

deposit over the earth. It comes into human society at certain points. Hence the world-wide demand cannot be concentrated on it. Any demand which does act on it can do so only by real transactions under price fluctuations. This fallacy, therefore, reminds us again of perpetual motion, wherein it is believed that we can get effect out of a force without action, reaction, and "escapement."

4. To meet another point somewhat more explicitly than I have done it above, let me say that if any nation which now uses gold finds that its interests are not served thereby, and thinks that silver would serve them better, it has only to make the experiment on its own risk and responsibility. If it succeeds, others will imitate it, and the inferences now made from the past action of nations will have to be modified. So far the nations have always acted as if they knew they were about to commit folly and incur loss whenever they have taken up any projects about silver, and they have insisted on first joining hands so as to all go into the evil together. We wait, then, for the first nation to give up gold and take silver because it thinks silver will serve its interest and convenience better. Mr. Gibbs is as anxious lest England should become a silver nation as any "gold monometallist" possibly could be.

5. If, then, we are asked which nations will take gold and which silver, and why any should take silver, and, if none take silver, where gold enough is to come from, we answer: (1) That it is not possible or necessary to tell *a priori* who will take silver and who gold. (2) All would prefer gold, and the world will probably ultimately come to use only a single universal standard of value, just as it probably will come to use single and universal standards of weights and measures. This, however, is only an anticipation which it must be left to time and the development of civilization to realize. At present it has no importance. If it is a correct anticipation it is fruitless; if it is an incorrect anticipation it is harmless. (3) If it is said that "there is not gold enough," that assertion is senseless unless we add: "to sustain prices and credits at their present level." If, then, there is not enough, in this sense, the nations will compete for gold until those to whom its advantages are worth most get it, because they give most (goods) for it. Others will

drop out of the competition for gold and take silver whenever its comparative cheapness more than counterbalances its inferior utility. So then, if there is not enough gold, we will use silver, and those will take some silver who think it for their interest, all things considered, so to do.

WAGES.

ONE may read, in scores of books and articles, that political economy is going through a transition stage. The inference appears to be that the period is a convenient one for any one who chooses to do so to contribute some crude notions to the prevailing confusion. It is certainly true that there is no body of economists engaged in carrying on the science of political economy by a consistent development of its older results according to such new light as can be brought to bear upon them. The science is exposed to the derision and flippant jests of those whose vested interest in old abuses is threatened by it, and it has forfeited its influence in the counsels of legislators and the cabinets of statesmen because those who call themselves economists are busy in turning economic science to scorn. Every science suffers more or less from men who meddle with it without mastering it, and from those who think carelessly, generalize rashly, or make concessions hastily; but a progressive science is always in the control, in the last resort, of a body of competent scholars who correct aberrations, and every such science possesses a body of criticism which is strong enough to repress presuming ignorance and charlatanism. Political economy is in no such position. A host of writers have been busy for the last twenty years introducing conflicting and baseless notions which, for want of a competent criticism, have won standing in the science. Others have made a boast of turning their backs on scientific method, and of describing, by way of contributing to political economy, some portion of the surface appearance which is presented by the mass of economic phenomena in their sequence, variety, and complexity. That is as if a historian should boast of abandoning the attempt to trace social forces in history, and of returning to the description of royal marriages and diplomatic intrigues. With all this the new school has been by no means moderate in its terms of contempt for all who did not accept the decree that Smith, Ricardo, and Mill were exceptional imbeciles to adopt and teach the old doctrines. I confess, for one, that for some years the writers of the new school imposed on me not a little by their airs of confidence and superiority. It seemed to me that I could perceive the errors into which they had fallen, the emptiness of their objections, the crude and unscientific character of their thinking; but I was forced to doubt and hesitate lest it might be I who was at fault.

For an example I will not take a small case or an extreme case. I will take an example of a very interesting and valuable book by one of the best living writers on political economy, but one who has, in my opinion, made unfounded and improper concessions on important economic doctrine. Leroy-Beaulieu[1] has not been able to escape the fascination of the longing for equality, and he declares his conclusion that Ricardo's doctrine of rent has no application at present because of the immense amount of new land which has become available, and that the Malthusian doctrine of population has no application because improvements in the arts are lowering the cost of subsistence in spite of the increase of population. Further on I shall notice some of the same writer's views about wages.

In the first place, the question What is true? is one thing, and the question of applicability to a given case is another. The former question is the one which is the concern of the scientific man. There is, however, another and more important view of the objections raised by the French economist.

In all our sciences we are forced to investigate ratios at the limit or other features of limiting cases. The older economists did this without having analyzed their processes sufficiently to classify them. The Ricardian law of rent is stated as a limiting case in the operation of the diminishing return from land. In any such statement the amount of land and the stage of the

[1] Essai sur la Répartition des Richesses et sur la Tendance à une Moindre Inegalité des Conditions, par Paul Leroy-Beaulieu. Paris: Guillaumin et Cie. 1881.

arts must be constant quantities. When the statement is derived from the limiting case it is used in political economy, as in all other sciences, by giving all values to the variables. Therefore the Ricardian law of rent applies to all cases whatsoever from Minnesota to Connaught. If we change the constants, either by getting more land or by advancing the arts, we produce no change whatever in the law, but only transfer its operation to another plane. As I regard it, M. Leroy-Beaulieu has fallen into the error of regarding a change in the constant as setting aside the law. The law of population is stated in terms of a limiting ratio between population and subsistence, land and the stage of the arts being constant. In its simplest terms the law is that the mortality and the increase of population are in equilibrium at the limit. M. Leroy-Beaulieu says that the law is set aside because we are not at the limit; but the law evidently covers all cases whatsoever, and to say that it does not apply is like saying that men are not under conditions of heat because they are not being either roasted or frozen. Whole libraries of books have been written, by way of criticism on the doctrines of political economy, whose argument consists in showing that human societies are rarely at the limit, or that limiting cases rarely or never occur. It seems to me, therefore, that the responsibility ought to be strictly enforced against men of standing in the science for concessions which introduce confusion, set the popularizers all astray, and make greater the task of those who are striving to secure the appreciation of sound doctrine. The men of the new school have scarcely met with any contradiction for the last ten years. They have had things all their own way. The effects of their teachings are to be met with in newspapers and popular writings. I am, however, one of those who believe that all this activity of the new school has been in the way of confusion and mischief. I do not doubt that we can to-day, with the aid of wider social philosophy and more careful study, expand and correct the doctrines of our science. We can advance it by an orderly and strictly genetic development. Any one who tries to advance it otherwise may be an apostle or a prophet; he is not a man of science.

I now propose to re-examine the subject of wages.

The origin of capital is lost in the obscurity which covers

the first beginnings of civilization. Some faint presages of capital are to be noted amongst brutes. We are told that a gorilla has been seen to take up a stick with which to defend himself when attacked. It is related that a monkey in a zoölogical garden used a stone to crack a nut, and hid the stone under the straw so as to have it ready on the next occasion. Beasts, however, with such extraordinary exceptions, live on the spontaneous products of the earth, which they consume as they find them, and which they obtain without tools or weapons. Such must also, at some time, have been the condition of man. In that stage of life alone could a man subsist on the immediate product of his labor. His labor consisted purely in an act of appropriation of the spontaneous fruits of the earth, which he consumed as he obtained them.

There is one tool-weapon given in nature—the flint; and there is one natural agent which man learned to use so early that we can find no period when it was not in use—fire. Accident was the leading factor in the earliest stage of civilization. All that we know of primitive men warns us not to believe that, if one man found a flint-knife, his comrades quickly took up the determination to acquire something of the same kind. The evidence all imposes upon us the conviction that the period during which the first steps towards capital, by the use of flints and fire, were being made must have been so long and painful that we cannot appreciate it. It is probable that steps forward were made only where population was dense enough to make effort necessary, and not dense enough to produce degeneration or distress. During that period the developments of rudimentary civilization must have been erratic and uncertain. Whenever any man or men, stimulated by perceiving the advantages which a man enjoyed who owned a flint-knife, and unable to conquer him and take it away from him, undertook to acquire one, not by accident but of set purpose, such persons were driven either to accumulate a store of food which would support life while searching for flints, or to go hungry while prosecuting that search. In either case the price of advance was the acquisition of capital by self-denial. From that stage of things up to the present moment it is true, leaving accident out of account, that *every step of advance by which man has raised himself above the level of other animals has been won by standing on a past self-denial, i.e. capital.* Capital is, like every other good, only a chance. Man may abuse it to his destruction or may use it for his advancement. That is where the moral deduction comes in, with which the economist has nothing to do, but the converse of the above proposition admits of absolute statement: Every diminution of capital lowers civilization without any possible alternative, and, in its measure, carries the race back towards the primitive barbarism. Labor and self-denial, to work yet abstain from enjoying, to earn a product yet work on as if one possessed nothing, have been the conditions of advance for the human race from the beginning, and they continue to be such still. From the beginning capital has been multiplied into itself in a constant involution. It is labor raised to a higher power and concentrated, and it is by this accumulation that man has gained the disposition of power enough, capable of concentration on a given point, to accomplish all his victories over nature. From the flint-knife up to the breech-loading rifle and the ocean steamer every step of the development is open to our observation, and not a single step in the sequence could be omitted or put in another position without making the result impossible.

The extension of our political economy which is most essential is the investigation of the element of *time*, and a specification of its value and relation in each of our generalizations. Already in the above sketch of the development of capital it is apparent that the relations of time are of the first importance. The work of mankind on low stages of civilization is irregular and unmethodical, but by the time that the agricultural stage is reached the successive periods of production repeat themselves with the regularity, because according to the necessity, of the seasons. Capital is the product of the past season. The work of the present season cannot go on without it, and it is not present unless the past period has been industriously employed. The future enjoyment, in its turn, depends on the industry of the present. The capital, moreover, in each period of production must be consumed; that is, used up and sacrificed. It must be sought again in the new product at the end of the present period of production, but in the interval it must be suffered to pass away and disappear. The element of risk therefore belongs to the nature of capital, and the work of mankind goes on in a series of pulsations in which the capital is consumed and sought again with increase in an endless series of reproductions.

On the hunting stage each man participates in the work and in the enjoyment. On the pastoral stage we already find cases in which men are left outside of any family connection and without cattle, the most essential form of capital. Such men, if not adopted into a family, and others who voluntarily take such a course, serve others who can give them a social status (security) and a share in the means of subsistence. In the early stages of the agricultural stage each man tills land for himself, and, so long as the land is abundant, new-comers simply take up more of it. In such a state of society, which is repeated substantially in all new countries, there is no class of persons who labor for others for hire. If any do this in their youth, or for a few years, they speedily acquire the small amount of capital necessary, in that stage of society, for tilling land, and become independent land-owners. As the population increases, however, the stage of the arts being assumed constant and land being taken constant in amount (viz., such an amount as is available for the use of a given society, whether it be, on that stage of the arts, a square mile or the whole earth), increments of subsistence must be won at greater cost of labor and sacrifice. The society is therefore forced to higher and higher organization because higher organization with differentiation of function increases production. As this movement goes on the society becomes more and more complex; the stake of each one in the stability of the organization is greater and greater, and whole classes arise which perform remote and incidental functions which would not exist at all in a less developed social system. In such a society a class of persons comes into existence who have no capital and no land. They must subsist from day to day out of the existing capital of the society by obtaining that capital from the owners of it through some form of voluntary agreement.

The English economists speak of the gain from the poorest land in cultivation as equal to current wages and profits. That they should have regarded wages and profits as positive data or known quantities is not strange in view of their situation and the circumstances of their country. There are in fact no positive data in economics from which results may be deduced as unknown are derived from known quantities. We have to accustom ourselves to think of the industrial system as in constant flux and readjustment. The elements of the system are numerous and are subject to constant variations in quantity and in their relations to each other. They are constantly moving, so that all forces which are produced in the system are distributed and taken up throughout the whole of it, so that every part is affected. A man of scientific training who studies society can no more doubt that this is true than he could doubt its truth as a general doctrine of the physical universe, altho society is more complex and its phenomena elude our investigation more completely. No doubt, taking a certain period, say a decade, into account, the existing ratio of product from the poorest land in cultivation to the labor and capital which must be expended on that land in the existing stage of the arts sets the general limit of the status of the lowest class of the population, from which the status of other classes is established in the proportion of what they contribute by their labor and capital to the total product of the country. In a new country where land can be tilled with a minimum of capital and a minimum organization of labor, any able-bodied man can obtain it and can win from it all the essentials of subsistence. To such a man the relation of wages to land is presented as an open alternative. There is no class, in such a country, of men who are driven, by the necessity of living, into a desperate competition with each other, without reserve, to get a share in the capital of the society. Women do compete with each other without the alternative. This is one of the chief reasons why their earnings are less than those of men in similar cases. In such a country there will be only an imperfectly differentiated wages class. The minimum of wages, where wages are paid, must be such as will give, all things considered, as good a return of comfort as can be won directly from the land. Since the latter return is great, wages must be high. Such is the state of the case at the present time in the United States. On the other hand, a country whose population is so great that the last increment of subsistence must be won from soils which require a great expenditure of labor and capital to win a meagre supply of the means of subsistence per head of the laborers must have a class of persons always on the verge of distress. As the use of such soils requires a large expenditure of capital, the laborers engaged upon it are employed by hire, and their status fixes a minimum of wages for manual labor.

Let us now vary the constants, the amount of land and the stage of the arts. It is plain that we immediately widen the margin of ease still further in the new country, and that we immediately relax the stringency of the situation in the old country. That is why civilization has advanced, and why we are now striving all the time to win progress in the arts. If the advance should be won as a single isolated step, it would bring relief for a time to all and an enlarged chance to all, but the law itself would not change at all; and if the population increased until it had absorbed all the advantage which had been won, the same results as before would be repeated. At the present time the unoccupied land of the earth is brought within such easy reach of all civilized men that there is no reason, save in the negligence of the classes interested themselves, why there should be any class of persons in the civilized world directly dependent on hire. The greatest mischief of all socialistic and semi-socialistic teaching is that it teaches the classes in question not to avail themselves by their own energy of the chances which are open to them, but to stay where they are and expect somebody else to make them happy there.

In a village community each man addressed himself directly to the soil to get out of it the means of subsistence. If then he failed for any reason whatsoever, he could only blame himself or nature. In our highly organized society we are all bound to each other in various relations while trying to win subsistence. The struggle for existence, therefore, which formerly had the character of a struggle of man with nature, now has the character of a struggle of man with man, and a "social question" arises whenever a man is dissatisfied with the return which he wins from the social co-operative effort. For instance: If a man were working by himself as a wheelwright and selling his wagons, he would have to put up with the best return which his labor and capital could win. If he could find any other trade which he could adopt and which would pay better, he would change. If, however, a capitalist employed wheelwrights and sold wagons, and if the trade should not bring back the capital and profits, the employer would either discharge men or lower wages. This is the form in which, under the social organization, the warning would come to the men that a redistribution of labor was required, but it would appear to them to be the act of the employer. Similar observations would hold of scores of other cases in which the ills of earthly life come to us as misdeeds of our neighbors towards us, on account of the relations in which we stand in the industrial organization.

Supply and demand, in the last analysis, are only so much need of subsistence and so many resources of subsistence, or, in other words, they are only the forms which are taken in the social organization by the original need of man addressed to nature on the one side, and the stores of nature open to the effort of man on the other. An isolated man would find the demand in his brain and the supply by his hand. When the supply had produced satisfaction the demand would arise again, and the reactions between the man and his environment would be repeated as long as he lived. In a primitive society a man who needed food exerted himself to get it from nature by some direct effort. A "just" return for his effort was—what he got. Under division of labor and exchange, even up to the last refinements of our modern industrial organization, it is still true that the society develops needs and addresses its efforts to nature to try to win satisfaction, but every man is forced to reach nature through a multitude of relations with his fellow-man. We stand in a double relation as suppliers and demanders around the one pile of goods which our organized effort has won from the earth and advanced into a shape to satisfy human needs. Hence every exchange involves two articles, each under two different relations. One article is supply to A and demand to B, while the other article is demand to A and supply to B. Hence demand and supply are the relations which bind men together into a human society for co-operation and high organization in a joint effort to win the supplies of life. The lowest terms to which any exchange can be reduced are therefore represented by two curves cutting each other; that is to say, by two simultaneous equations between two variables. Even then we have only a representation of an instantaneous transaction. If we take into account successive transactions and variations in supply and demand, we must introduce the element of time. We should then have to use the third dimension to represent the case, and after all we should have only an empirical, statistical, or, as we might call it, a statical, representation of supply and demand. If we should attempt any analysis of supply and demand regarded dynamically, we should also have to use the element of time; and if we made such an attempt, we should find ourselves doomed to inevitable failure. It is not possible to analyze supply and demand. Why does A offer wheat for $1 and B bid only 99 cts. for it? These are secrets of the consciousness of the parties. One or both of them may be led by considerations which are erroneous. That will not affect the influence of his bid on the market. The economist can do no more than to note the bid when it is made as a contribution to the making of the price. The reasons for it he cannot discover. The most that he can do towards the analysis of supply and demand is to study the facts and circumstances which, by general tendency, go to make the supply of a given commodity, or the demand for it, greater or smaller. Indeed this is the only thing which it is of importance for us to know. Supply and demand are together the ultimate force or fact to the economist. They are to him what gravity is to the astronomer or chemical affinity to the chemist. We want to know the mode of their action, but the reason of it is beyond our reach. Supply and demand act to clear the market. If there were a closed market and a sale without reserve, supply and demand would just distribute all the commodities on the market. Supply and demand would not give each person what he would like to have, nor satisfy any ideal desires, any more than a man who addresses himself directly to nature in the first instance gets what he would like to have, but, if they act freely, supply and demand distribute commodities so that a given amount shall produce a maximum of satisfaction to the community between whose members the exchanges are made. At that point supply and demand would be in equilibrium and no further transactions would be made. In a simple society, with exchanges at country fairs, this state of things was reached. In our modern society, in which production, exchange, and consumption never cease, the conditions of the market constantly change and never cease, so that supply and demand move on towards an equilibrium which is never realized because the conditions of it are constantly changed. What then is "justice" in this connection? The distribution which takes place under the free play of supply and demand gives us our definition of justice as applied to the contribution which an individual puts into the social effort and the share he gets out of the social product. There is no other definition of justice which can be seriously considered.

There are two sources of confusion which must now be corrected.

1. The first is the definition of wages. If wages mean the remuneration of labor, then wages are a chief class, and we must distinguish between payment by the piece, contract wages, deferred wages, store pay, etc. etc., as sub-classes. If we make the definition of wages to fit contract wages, then the remuneration of labor will be a chief class, and we must distinguish between wages, payment by the piece, store pay, etc. etc., as sub-classes. Either classification is legitimate if it is faithfully observed throughout, but if any ambiguity is allowed to creep in it will produce the logical errors of a double definition and confusion between a chief class and a sub-class. These logical errors run through a great deal of the controversial literature about wages, and when they are cleared away a great part of the controversy falls to the ground. The second of the above classifications is by far the best, because it allows of a definition of wages which conforms to the popular use of the term. *Wages are a payment per unit of time by the employer, in return for which the employee agrees to use his productive powers during the time specified as the employer may direct.* I use the word under this definition only.

2. In the works of Mill and the other authorities there is a confusion as to the source from which wages are paid which is, I think, one chief cause of all the controversy which has arisen on this subject. It is distinctly taught under the head of wages that the demand for labor is capital, and that wages are paid out of *capital.* Under the head of distribution it is said that the *product* is divided into wages, profits, and rent, from which it

would follow that wages are paid out of product. Leroy-Beaulieu describes the employment of *capital* to sustain labor during production with great minuteness (pp. 366–70), and then declares summarily that the only "wage-fund" is "the total annual *production* minus what is necessary to maintain capital" (p. 382). Ricardo held that profits and wages are the leavings of each other. Later economists have generally rejected this doctrine, but even those of them who maintain that wages are paid out of capital fall back into arguments which imply its truth. For instance, Cairnes, who earnestly maintained that capital is divided into wages, raw material, and fixed capital, argued that trades-unions could not increase the wages in the several trades, because, if they did so, they would reduce profits below the rate which would make investment worth while. On his own doctrine, increased wages could not trench on profits. He should have argued that wages, if increased by a trades-union, could only be increased at the expense of raw material or fixed capital, which would be far more difficult than to increase them at the expense of profits. Indeed if the trades-union movement did not coincide with a new distribution of capital into its three parts (a new distribution which would produce a rise in wages), the trades-union could not possibly force an advance at the expense of raw materials or fixed capital. We shall see further on that wages and profits are not the leavings of each other, because they are not parts of the same whole.

If we could arrest the production and consumption of wealth in the United States at a given moment of time and take an inventory of all the wealth at that moment existing, it is evident that it would be an exact arithmetical quantity. It would be what the combined industry, economy, extravagance, folly, and idleness of all past time on the part of the American people had made it. It would be less because we have had a civil war, a protective tariff, a paper-money crisis, fires at Chicago and Boston, etc. etc., than it would have been if our public policy had been wiser and our misfortunes less. Whatever the existing wealth might be, no regrets could carry us back to increase it by a grain of wheat or a pound of iron beyond what it was at the moment supposed. This wealth would be divided by its character and by the disposition of it which was intended by the persons who owned it, in the then beginning period of production, into fixed capital, raw material, and supplies for the support of laborers. In one country, like England, the industrial system might be such that the support of laborers would nearly all be distributed in wages. In that case the term "wage-fund" might with great propriety be applied to it as a technical term to avoid a circumlocution. In another country, like the United States, the supplies for the support of labor might be, for the most part, owned by yeomen farmers and other independent laborers, or they might be distributed by other modes of remunerating labor than wages. A laborer may own a farm and support himself while working, and wait for his pay until the work is done. He then advances part of the capital and is not strictly a laborer only. He may take "store-pay." In that case he also advances part of the capital of the enterprise, and he goes into the market to borrow that capital, paying very heavy discount rates for it. These cases cannot throw any light on wages. They have to be noted only to eliminate them from the consideration of wages. The wages system exists, as above shown, only where the ratio of population to land is such that a class is differentiated which, having no capital or land, is dependent day by day for support on a contract relation with those who have capital. We have also seen that, above the very lowest stage of life, capital must precede and be the means to every productive effort.

In the actual period of production then, on a wages system, the existing supplies for laborers are distributed to laborers in wages while they, with the help of the fixed capital, till the ground and work up the raw materials, transforming the old capital into a new product. The risk, as we have seen, belongs to capital, and the great advantage of the wages system is that it leaves the risk all on capital. The laborer works by *time*, and when the time is over his contract is fulfilled. He takes no risk or responsibility. He is therefore at liberty to address himself to the accumulation of capital in the simplest possible manner, by economy of his wages, undisturbed by other elements. His share in the business lasts during the period of production and ends with it. He has no claim or right in the product, for he sold his share in producing it and took his pay for it during the process. The product is divided at the end of the period of production into the replacement of the capital (support of laborers, raw material, and wear of fixed capital), profits, and rents. As the capital to be replaced belonged to the capitalist, all the replacement goes to him together with the profits. Rent goes to the land-owner. The products are next distributed by supply and demand amongst all the members of the society, who turn them into capital and divide them, according to their good judgment, into the same parts as before, the product of the last period perhaps becoming the raw material of the next, and another period of production is then begun. If the product and profit of the last period were large, the accumulation of capital will be large—that is, the stock of supplies for laborers in the next period will be great; but it is not until the next period, and after an increase of capital, that any effect on wages can be produced. Hence it is clear that wages and profits are not parts of the same whole. Wages were in capital at the beginning of the period of production; profits are in the product at its close. We cannot establish any equation between the wages and the total capital, or the profits and the total product, or the total capital and the total product. How then can we establish an equation between wages and profits so as to determine the effect on one of variations in the other?

When now we have thus analyzed the operation in detail of the constant action and reaction by which the industrial functions of society are carried on, it is immaterial what may be the speed at which the process goes forward, or what may be the varieties of detail in different industries. Nothing can alter the nature or sequence of the forces and effects. The effect of credit to economize time and synchronize certain steps changes nothing in the scientific analysis of the process. It is a separate complication and refinement to be studied by itself.

Four inferences may be drawn immediately.

(1) We see that all questions whether the laborer gets his share of the product or not are, under the wages system, nonsensical. (2) That the appeal, often made in England, to workmen to take lower wages, so that the English products can be sold cheaper in foreign markets, are founded on false conceptions of wages, and ought to have no weight. (3) That the

arguments of the American protectionists, drawn from comparative rates of wages, are all fallacious. (4) That the attempt to connect wages with the price of products, by a sliding scale or otherwise, is founded on no true relations, and is doomed to failure. If an employer should say to his men, "My business is not prosperous like that of my neighbors. I want you to work for me for $2 a day, altho the market rate which you could get is $2.25,"—he would not deserve a respectful reply. Neither is there any sense at all in the demand of the men, if they say to the employer, "Your business is exceptionally prosperous, and we want you to give us $2.25, altho the market rate which we could get elsewhere is $2."

The notion that wages ever can be paid out of product is the most ridiculous notion which has ever been introduced into political economy. It would mean that a man who was tilling the ground in June could eat the crop he expected to have in September, or that a tailor could be wearing the coat which he was making. Men could then eat their intentions, wear their hopes, and be warmed by their promises. Even more than this: they might then believe that regrets were no longer vain, and having borrowed the future they could recall the past. The man who has been industrious to-day has a supper to-night. The man who has been idle to-day is hungry to-night. If wages can be paid out of product, the latter man, in his hunger, penitence, and regret, might as well obtain a loaf advanced from nature on credit to-night as to get one at any other time before he has won it by labor. He could then eat and sleep, and in the morning he could break his promise to nature and refuse to produce the loaf. Whenever nature yields to man an atom which he has not earned, or advances it one second of time before he has earned it, we may all turn socialists and utopists. The real gist of the question about wages lies right here. The "wage-fund" is of no importance one way or another. Every one who has yielded to sentimental faiths or longings to lessen the hardships of getting a living, or to discover some way by which men may attain to happiness except by conquering it, has seen himself forced to attack the doctrine that wages are paid out of capital.

Some instances of the fallacy about wages which has just been exposed are worth analyzing. In the July number of the

PRINCETON REVIEW Mr. Carroll D. Wright gives two cases which he makes the basis of deduction on the doctrine that wages are paid out of capital. The first case is stated thus:

> "The workers are often the direct cause of the reduction in wages. This is well illustrated by circumstances within my observation. A well-known and prosperous dealer in boots and shoes in one of our large shoe towns is very popular with the workingmen because he will sell them a pair of boots for a quarter less than the same quality can be purchased elsewhere. It does not occur to them that they have paid that discount, but they complain to their employers who have cut them down—a cut-down required in order to furnish the popular dealer with goods at a low price to enable him to undersell smaller dealers. This retail dealer obtains from the manufacturer his lowest price for making one hundred cases as per sample. He then offers to pay so much—a sum less than the manufacturer's estimate—and pay cash. The manufacturer rather than lose a good cash order consents to make the goods, but not being able to reduce the cost of raw material takes the discount out of labor, and the workman berates the employer for reducing his wages while he praises the dealer for selling him his boots at a low price. Such circumstances often exist."

The inference which we are invited to make is that the workmen were foolish to buy where they could buy most cheaply because they thereby caused their own wages to be reduced.

In the first place, is the case correctly observed? If so, the employer-manufacturer sold goods by favoritism to one dealer who lowered his price to *all* his customers, and the employer lowered his wages for *all* his production so that his men had less to spend for *all* objects of their desire. The employer, therefore, in the last analysis, took something from his men and gave part of it to the general public of the vicinity and kept part himself, while his men lost on their wages what they gained on their shoes and more too. No one can regard such a statement as correct who has any conception of economic laws and relations. The true facts lie on the face of the statement. The reduction in price to the retailer came out of interest and insurance against bad debts, because it was given for cash. It did not have any connection at all with wages. It is to be assumed that the manufacturer would have given similar terms to any retailer who would have paid cash. Otherwise he would have been guilty of favoritism which would have ruined his business.

If wages were reduced, that act could not have had any connection at all with the fact that the employer had allowed to one customer a reduction for cash. Were, then, the men wise to profit by the reduction? Undoubtedly they were. Mr. Wright is driven by his view of the matter into the venerable fallacy that we get rich by what we spend, not by what we save, or that a demand for commodities is a demand for labor. That is really the fallacy at the bottom of all the unsound views of wages, but it is a certain extension of it to hold that the way for the men to make their wages large is themselves to demand a great many of their own products; that is, to spend their money freely.

Mr. Wright's second case is this:

"The day-laborer feeling himself more of a man than formerly must oftener wear a white laundered shirt, but he cannot pay over fifty cents for one. The demand of the higher civilization of the day-laborer must be met, and white laundered shirts are supplied at retail for fifty cents, and even for thirty-seven cents. But the wages of the women who make them have been reduced to eight cents per shirt. All such illustrations are simple, but well adapted to show the workingman what is meant by wages being paid from the product of labor, and in accordance with the profit which may be expected from the sale of the product."

What effect this proof of the effect of paying wages out of product may have on the laborer I cannot say, but I should think that it might arrest the economist by some misgivings as to his dogma. The fixed fact, the known quantity, in this case is "the demand of the higher civilization of the day-laborer." The day-laborer appears to be in command of the situation. He decides that he wants a white laundered shirt and that he only wants to pay fifty cents for it. Considering that he is the first man in the history of the human race who has ever been in a position to make his wants the law of his satisfactions, he certainly is moderate. As it is, his demand is satisfied by cutting the sewing-women down to eight cents wages. He might have called for shirts at a cent apiece, in which case the sewing-woman must have seen her wages reduced to two or three mills. He might have demanded boots at twenty-five cents, coats at fifty cents, cigars ten for a cent, and so on, and the wages of bootmakers, tailors, and cigar-makers must have come down in obedience to the law that wages come out of product, to the proper figure to satisfy his demand. Mr. Wright would be forced to argue that the way for the wages class to improve their condition is to buy each other's products freely at generous prices. I am a day-laborer myself. My higher civilization demands that I have a saddle-horse for five dollars and a cottage at Newport for a hundred dollars. If wages are paid out of product, I presume that, now that I have published my wishes, they will be gratified not later than next summer. As for horse-breeders and builders, let them look to their wages. I should like the cottage furnished.

The wild and untrained writers on political economy perform one useful function. They seize on all the fallacies and, naïvely and with good faith, perpetrate the *reductio ad absurdum.* Mr. George holds that wages are paid out of product, and that they are a portion only of the laborer's own product which the employer gives back to him. If this is true, it suggests three questions: 1. What is the difference between a slave and a wage-receiver? 2. Why is any man an employee? 3. Why is not every man an employer?

The rate of wages is determined, like every other case of value, by supply and demand. The total capital will be divided between wages, raw material, and capital by supply and demand. Capital, however, is limited by its nature with respect to the extent to which it may be transferred from one of these divisions to the other. From period to period the capital, when reproduced, is transformed into one or the other class by the dynamical operation of supply and demand.

From period to period changes in the arts, in the industrial development, in national habits, in fashion as to co-operation, etc. etc., will alter the proportion between the amount of capital paid in wages and the amount used to support laborers under other industrial organizations. The supply of laborers in one or the other mode of industry will also vary. Capital is divided between the wages system and other systems by supply and demand.

Changes in fashion, art, science, education, etc., will alter the relative importance of non-competing groups in industry. General changes will also affect the number of laborers in each of the non-competing groups. Capital is divided between the non-competing groups by supply and demand.

Inside of any one group the capital of that group will be distributed (in the absence of trades-union rules or other interferences) by supply and demand, according to the demand and supply of personal talents and capacities.

Some have inferred from the application of supply and demand to wages that the problem of wages was a simple case of a ratio, so much capital to so many men. The error here lies in applying a mathematical relation which is far too simple for the facts of the case. I have stated above what is the simplest mathematical form of an exchange under supply and demand. Obviously it is a great error to treat it as a simple ratio of arithmetical quantities, or even as a ratio of variables.

Others have turned away from the application of supply and demand with impatience. The Germans like to say of it that it is *nichtssagend*. Some of them put "law" in quotation when they speak of it. Any one who can sneer at supply and demand or regard it as a barren formula has certainly failed to understand it, or to study the scope and subtlety of its action. No one has ever analyzed supply and demand, regarded dynamically, because no one can. Leroy-Beaulieu says: "We cannot affirm that this formula [supply and demand] is false. We ought only to say that it is philistine and commonplace. It is certainly true, as Cobden said, that when two bosses run after one workman wages rise, and when two workmen run after one boss wages fall; but this sort of truism is not fitted to satisfy strict thinkers. What are the circumstances which determine the demand and the supply?" This last question he does not answer, nor even attempt to answer. It seems to me that a strict thinker proves himself by recognizing an ultimate scientific fact or law when he comes to it. The more one studies, the more one finds that the results of all studies are truisms. One is astonished that he did not see at once, by pure common-sense, the highest and last result of laborious investigation. If there is anything philistine and commonplace, it is to set aside the results of study as "truisms," and to pursue questions which can only lead off again into a maze of unclassified phenomena. Further on the same author says that in addition to the supply and demand of labor we must take into account the fecundity of capital. He urges that the demand for labor is a function not simply of the amount of capital, but also of its organization and activity. But in any given period of production any new activity or improved application of capital cannot act upon the wages during that period. The advantage will appear in the product of that period, it will swell the capital of the next period and then act upon wages. He then adds: "It is not proper to say simply, The more capital increases relatively to population, the more do wages rise. This proposition would be either inexact or incomplete, for the productive force may advance far more rapidly than the accumulation of material capital." This objection is not sound. If productive force increases, it immediately produces more capital. That is the proof that it has increased, and the mode in which the gain from increased force is realized. Advance in productive power is therefore followed by increase of capital within an interval of at least one period of production, altho further increase of capital, due to the same development of productive power, may continue to advance in a geometrical ratio through a long series of subsequent periods. New machines produce quick and approximately uniform increase of capital. Education or better government produce slower returns, which advance at a high ratio through a long period. The same author then comes to the "true formula" which he proposes "after having set aside the formulas and inflexible notions of the principal economists:" "The more production increases relatively to population, the greater is the chance that wages may rise." We have here a capital example of the necessity of separating the element of *time* in economic problems, and subjecting it to special study. We set out to find a formula for what determines the rate of wages, which is always a fact of a given time and place. We are offered a formula of the conditions of change in that fact between one time and another. Let us try a parallel. It is asked, What determines the weight of a man? The answer is, Gravity acting on the mass of his body. No, M. Leroy-Beaulieu would say, that is a formula or inflexible dogma of the principal physicists. The weight of a man is determined by the fact that, if he has a good constitution, good health, good diet, obeys hygienic rules, does not work too hard, loses no limb by accident, etc. etc., his weight may increase from one time to another. Such errors would be impossible in any science but political economy, but recent economic literature is largely made up of just such confused thinking and reasoning. The rate of wages is the rate at which services are exchanged for means of subsistence under free contract and competition. It is therefore determined by supply and demand, like price, rate of interest, rate of foreign exchange, and all other cases of value.

We find therefore that there never ought to have been any "question" about wages at all, any more than there should have been a question about raw material or fixed capital. It is all wasted energy to re-analyze the subject and expose the fallacies which have been introduced by incompetent meddlers in economic science, encouraged by the concessions of the economists. Wages do not belong in distribution at all. They belong in the application of capital to production. The capitalist-employer is led by self-interest to try to keep wages down just exactly as he tries to prevent waste of raw material or wear and tear of fixed capital. The employee is led by self-interest to try to get all the wages he can. The struggle is legitimate and necessary. The result of it is that supply and demand distribute the capital amongst the laboring wage-receivers in the proportion which conduces to the maximum of production under all the existing circumstances. If trades-unions or employers' associations introduce interferences they may temporarily disturb this adjustment, but all such interferences avenge themselves in the end by compensating reactions. If a man knows how to earn more than he is getting, he ought to insist on getting more where he is or he should change. If an employer can get an equally competent man at lower wages, he ought to get him or lower wages. If we depart at all from this rule, we entangle ourselves in an endless muddle of sentimental rubbish, we lower production, and contract the welfare of all. There is therefore no "social question," or struggle of class with class, involved in wages. The notion that there is under "distribution" some new and unexplored field of economic science is entirely without foundation. That notion threatens to bring political economy still further under the dominion of metaphysics and sentiment, by the introduction of some notion of "justice," derived *aliunde*, as a controlling conception in economical science. It is indeed painful to think what an immense amount of poetry and declamation is swept away when we once get at the truth of the relations with which we have been dealing. If these relations were correctly understood, it would be impossible to make people any longer applaud the orator who finds it unjust that an industrious man is better off than a lazy one, or who wants a revolution because the man who has won capital by self-denial gets more luxurious living for himself and his children than the man who has spent as he went along. We should, however, have more sober industry and manly effort on the part of free, independent, and intelligent laborers to win capital and to put themselves and their children in a better position. There is no reason at all, at this moment, barring disease and accident, why any man living should not acquire capital, and, in view of the progress in the arts, there is no reason to apprehend, as far in the future as we can see, that this chance will not become rather greater than less for all who are prudent, industrious, and frugal, and who will turn their backs on the social doctors who have patent schemes for making everybody happy by setting those-who-have-not to rob those-who-have.

THE ARGUMENT AGAINST PROTECTIVE TAXES.

THE most absurd assertion which can be put into language is that a thing (*e.g.*, free trade) is true in theory but is false in practice. For, if free trade is not true in practice, something else, viz., restricted trade, is alleged to be true and beneficial in practice. It will therefore be a matter of scientific investigation to find out how restriction acts, what forces it brings into action, what are the laws of those forces, what are the conditions of successful restriction, etc. etc.—in short, to find out the theory and philosophy of restriction. The theory thus found will be "true" because deduced from observation and ratified by experience. But it was conceded, at the outset, that free trade is true in theory. Hence it would follow, if free trade is true in theory but not in practice, that two opposite and contradictory propositions about the same subject-matter could both be true at the same time. This is the height of absurdity. Any one, therefore, who makes this assertion is either guilty of very loose thinking, or else he seeks an escape, at all hazards, from rational conclusions against which he can no longer contend.

There remain two possible positions which a protectionist may assume:

1. He may boldly declare that there is a science of wealth based on restriction; that he can discover the principles of it and reduce them to a theory; that trade between countries is a mischievous thing, at least if it runs on parallels of latitude; that isolation and antagonism of nations is the law of nature upon which wealth and civilization depend; that there is therefore no universal science of wealth, but only a national science of wealth, and that this science, in its final analysis, is only a generalization from certain empirical maxims of economic policy. This is the

position of the dogmatic or philosophical protectionists, who seek to give a certain abstract and philosophical cast to their speculations. It is the position of the List-Carey school, whose "unscientific science and unhistorical history" (as Roscher called it) seems to impose with such weight on some people. It is a view of the matter which is especially cultivated now by the learned protectionists of Germany, and which issues in some of the most remarkable curiosities of economic literature which have ever been produced either by the learned or the unlearned.

2. The other ground which the protectionist may take is that protection does not increase wealth, but is, for some reason or other, expedient.

In taking up again now the effort to put into simple, brief, and comprehensive form the argument against protection, I will separate these two modes of defending protection and take them in order. It is obvious that the two positions are inconsistent with each other, and every one who is familiar with the history of this controversy knows that its fruitlessness has been due, in a large measure, to the ambiguities, false definitions, and confusion which have prevailed in it. It has been a constant phenomenon in the discussion that the expediency of protection, in spite of the harm done by it, has been argued, and then the general utility of protection has been assumed as resulting from the argument. I do not know of any disputant on the protectionist side who does not move from one to the other of these positions, as his convenience or the pressure of the argument may force him, or who does not confuse them with each other.

It will be noted also that my point of attack is *protection* under any form or in any degree, and not import duties or taxes on consumption. This distinction can perhaps best be brought out by examining one of the peculiar and whimsical notions which avail to keep people from actually examining the matter in issue, viz., the notion of "revenue tariff with incidental protection." The people who believe that this jingle of words has any meaning in it must believe that the same man in supplying his needs does it at the same time in two ways, by importing and by buying at home too. If A wants a ton of iron and imports it, he pays duties on it which go to the public treasury. Not a cent for this transaction goes to the American producer of iron. This is why the American producer is so often heard to cry out in horror at the amount imported. If B wants a ton of iron and buys it at home, he pays the protective taxes to the home producer, and not a cent goes in revenue to the public treasury for that transaction. What incidental relation exists between these two transactions? They are independent and exclusive of each other. If we discard the empty formula of "revenue with incidental protection," we find that we are simply face to face with the problem of free trade *vs.* protection, or revenue *vs.* protection, as in the first place. Nothing has been done by this formula towards solving either of those problems. A only wanted one ton and took one way of getting it. B only wanted one ton and took another way of getting it. The question why either of them chose the course he did choose, and what the effects were on the interests of either of them, and on the welfare of the country, of the tax laws in question, remains still all before us. What is clear is only that protection and revenue are exclusive of each other. They do not overlap each other at all. The line between them is sharp and precise, and we can discuss the wisdom of protection entirely aside from the wisdom of raising revenue from customs duties. The latter question shall not therefore now be taken into account, and we confine our attention only to the former.

In this connection we may also dispose of another of the glib commonplaces by which people get rid of the trouble of thinking about the tariff controversy: that we have a large debt and therefore must have a high (protective) tariff. It is evident, since protection and revenue exclude each other, that not one cent which is paid in a protective tax goes into the public treasury or helps to pay either the principal or the interest of the debt, while, on the other hand, every cent paid in protective taxes lessens the power of the citizen to pay revenue taxes for the discharge of the public burdens. Hence the fact that we have heavy public burdens is just the reason why we cannot afford to squander our means in paying taxes to our neighbors for carrying on (as they themselves allege) unproductive industries. The especial iniquity of the present tariff, in a political point of view, is that it was laid under the cover of war taxes, taking advantage of the popular ignorance of the relation between protection and revenue, and of the popular willingness to submit to taxation for the purpose of the war. To argue that we want protective taxes because we have a large debt to pay is like arguing that a man ought to squander his income in benevolence because his means are just now being strained by an expensive lawsuit.

Having disposed of these notions which interfere with the approach to the real merits of the question, we may consider first whether protection can increase the wealth of the country.

I. The problem of economic science is presented in the ratio between the efforts which men have to exert to supply their material needs and the amount and excellence of the food, clothing, lodging, furniture, fuel, etc., which they obtain. Political economy investigates the laws which govern this ratio so as to find out how we may determine the ratio as much as possible in our favor. Throwing aside all technicalities, the case is to find out how, for a given exertion and sacrifice, to get the maximum of material good. I maintain against any system of restriction whatsoever that it renders that ratio less favorable to men than it would be under freedom, taking the arts and sciences, the land and the population, as they are in the country where restriction is applied. Instead of increasing wealth, it is mathematically demonstrable that it lessens wealth, makes it harder to get a living and lowers the comfort of the population, and that it does this by taking away one man's earnings to give them to another. I mean to say that a man must work harder and longer to get a given amount of product under protection than under free trade, and I mean to say that this state of things is due to the statute law, which steps in and takes away part of his product and gives it to another man. The issue is purposely stated here without the use of any of the technical terms of political economy, because the simpler and homelier the language is the more correctly does it state the question, both in its economic and its political aspects, both in its scientific and in its popular significance, free from all admixture of either sentimental or pedantic rubbish. The economic question about the tariff is: Does it enable the population of the country to command greater material good for a given effort? The political question about protection is: Does the statute enacted by the legislature alter the distribution of property so that one man enjoys another man's earnings? Has the state a law in operation which enables one citizen to collect taxes of another? The scientific question about protection is: Does it lessen the ratio of effort and sacrifice to comfort and enjoyment? The popular question about protection is: Does it prevent me from supporting myself and family, by my labor, as well as I could do it if there were no protective taxes?

The philosophical protectionists at once reply that this is not the question, or at least not the whole of it. To them political economy is not an independent science. They are not willing to consider the question of wealth aside from other things. They want to embrace in the view what they call moral, political, social, æsthetical, and sentimental considerations. Their instinct is perfectly correct when they oppose those operations of analysis and classification which would introduce clearness and precision into the discussion. The part of social science which has the most positive and mathematical character is the one against which they cannot stand. They write no books on political economy, but always on social science, in order to keep the clear mixed with the unclear, the physical with the metaphysical, the positive with the arbitrary. They are eagerly followed by all the popular orators and writers on economic questions, and generally by those metaphysicians and students of other sciences who take part in sociological discussions, and almost always prove themselves the most reckless dogmatizers when they do so. The attraction of the *a priori* method, and of abstract and general propositions for ill-trained men, is well known, and, generally, in proportion as one is untrained in a particular science (whatever may be his status in others) will be his readiness to fly to *a priori* methods and to dogmas which are conveniently vague, loose, and broad, when he engages in the discussion of questions appertaining to the science in which he has not been trained.

Mr. Carey, for instance, filled his books with vague diatribes about "association." He thought to have found a great principle under this name. He wanted to break off all the natural ties and bonds of mankind in order to piece the parts together again on a plan of his own. He accordingly wrote big books on "social science," and he never reached the first conception of the forces which may truly be called social, or the laws by which they act. He and his school, in this country and in Germany, have never learned to see the great bonds of human society which are developed by intercourse and communication, which hold the nations to a mutual giving and taking as they grow in civilization, which are stronger in proportion as they are natural, informal, impersonal, spontaneous, and in comparison with which all artificial co-operation is ridiculously insignificant. For our present purpose, however, the thing to note is that social speculations and sociological investigations have nothing whatever to do with the tariff for protection. They only obscure and confuse the tariff question. If we should classify them we should find that they are either broader generalizations which flow necessarily from sound economic principles, and so can be left to take care of themselves while the economic investigations are going on; or else they are sociological doctrines which are parallel with sound economic doctrines, but which are most successfully pursued in special investigations; or else (which is by far the largest class) they are sentimental whims, popular notions, and metaphysical dogmas, which are not true, or at best are only half true, but which cannot be refuted without allowing the discussion to fritter itself away in innumerable side issues. We have to understand that an economic investigation may be carried on just as independently as a chemical or physical or biological investigation. The economist does not need to be on the lookout all the time to correct his results by reference to some outside considerations, or to the dogmas of jejune and rickety systems of metaphysical speculation. On the contrary, he should regard the introduction of extraneous elements, no matter under what high-sounding names, of moral, political, and social, as sure signs of impending confusion and fallacy, and he should especially repel any attempt to measure and criticise his results by the facile generalizations of *a priori* speculation. So much being here briefly set out, we may devote ourselves to the question of protection as a question of wealth and political economy only, as above described.

Let us take the case of a new country. It is claimed that a new country needs protection in order to get a start. Mill seemed to make some concession to this case. I have heard a man who was not a protectionist and who was a professional economist say that he thought a new colony might get into a situation in which it might need a lift to move it on in the way of growth. I will take up this latter view of the matter for discussion because it is the case which, if disproved, will *a fortiori* carry all the other forms of this claim with it.

I pass over the practical difficulty involved in the question who is to decide when the juncture supposed has come about, and who is to prescribe or give the lift; I pass over the unscientific and incorrect conception of econonic forces involved in the hypothesis that a nation can get into any such position, and also in the notion of a "lift" to be given to a nation, in order that I may come to the real test of the remedy proposed, if the case could arise, and if the remedy were practically available. It is evident that a protective tariff cannot render any foreign capital or labor available to help the nation which lays the tariff. If a nation lays import duties for revenue some part of them may fall on the foreigner, but if it lays such duties for protection it keeps foreign goods out. If, then, the foreigner stays at home and is forced to keep his goods at home, the protecting country cannot make use of him or his goods in any way whatever to suit its ends or avert its misfortunes. Whatever effect the protective taxes exert must be exerted in the protecting country, on its own labor and capital. Any favor or encouragement which the protective system exerts on one group of its population must be won by an equivalent oppression exerted on some other group. To suppose the contrary is to deny the most obvious application of the conservation of energy to economic forces. If the legislation did not simply transfer capital it would have to make capital out of nothing. Now the transfer is not simply an equal redistribution; there is loss and waste in the case of any tax whatsoever. There is especial loss and waste in the case of a protective tax. We cannot collect taxes and redistribute them without loss; much less can we produce forced monopolies and distorted industrial relations without loss. It follows then that if a nation could come into some temporary industrial compression or arrested growth, a protective tariff not only would not help it out, but would contribute to still further limit its powers of self-development and to restrain its recuperative energies.

We have then reduced the issue which we are discussing to such terms that, after analyzing the phenomena, we are able to test the protectionist theory by universal canons of science, and we have a mathematical demonstration that protection is a delusion, which, like bimetallism, fiat money, socialism, and utopianism, is an attempt to make something out of nothing, or to create energy by law.

Here we shall be met, however, by the people who insist on believing that a better organization of labor, or greater activity of labor, or some other advantage which is real altho not specific, more than offsets the injury, or that the injured ones participate again in some vague gain. It is very singular that the people who believe in these notions are so slow to understand the fact that whatever lessens the wealth of a community, in the widest generalization or deduction only lessens its wealth! and cannot possibly increase it, and that the result is either to lessen the wealth *per capita*, or, if some do not become poorer, then others must be rendered still more poor. The protective tariff must act on people who without it would distribute their industry according to the chances of the greatest profit. The tariff is needed, by the protectionist hypothesis, in order to counteract the distribution which is thus brought about. But the tariff itself can appeal to no motive save that of desire for profit. It does so by providing that a certain industry shall, under protection, pay higher profits than it could under freedom, and it expects that this inducement will operate to make labor and capital seek this industry. If then desire for profit was not a sufficient and wise guide under freedom, what makes it such under protection? The notion that the legislature has a wisdom greater than that of the people, and can point out the industries they ought to pursue, has often been refuted; but the protective theory really assumes more than that. It assumes that the law can enlighten the desire for profit, and make it a more trustworthy guide than it would be under freedom. In truth there is nothing at all wanted in the cases to which protection is applied but capital, which the law can never produce. The efficiency of the tariff is that it does get this capital—from other people. The rest is all phrases intended to occupy attention while the thimblerig is going on. If this is not so, let some protectionist analyze the operation of his system, and show by reference to undisputed economic principles where and how it exerts any effect on production to increase it. Customs sometimes grow up under the efforts of men to bring about arrangements which will be convenient for industry and commerce. The law can often follow these customs, recognize them, and give them positive form. Institutions grow out of needs, and to meet purposes, to which institutions the law can give form and sanction. I know of nothing more than this which the law can do for industry.

What has been proved now of a new country holds true all the more of an old one. The only difference is that a new country may endure protection while an old one cannot. A new country which produces, as all new countries do, food and raw materials may create parasite industries to live on the exuberant productions of its natural industries, and on the special advantage in exchange which a new country has when it exchanges food and raw materials for finished products. An old country cannot exclude food and raw materials. In a new country the burden of the tariff system falls on the superfluity of the people —superfluity not in respect to what they would like to have, but in comparison with what people in old countries have. In an old country there are large classes of persons who are at best on the verge of poverty, and who are forced to labor hard and for long hours to win subsistence. Taxes on food and raw materials would crush these classes down to misery. Germany is trying it with a tariff which is quite insignificant compared with ours. What I have proved, therefore, with regard to the effect of a protective tariff in a new country holds *a fortiori* in an old country, and is true universally. A restricted trade lowers the physical well-being of the population, and, with that, all chance of intellectual and moral well-being, below what it would be under free trade, with the same conditions of labor, capital, and land.

II. I go on then to consider the other protectionist position: that protection is not a means of wealth, but is temporarily expedient.

Under this head the controversy has rambled over the whole field of economic speculation, embracing also all history and all statistics, and here also the vague sentimental and metaphysical considerations have had the greater scope, as this is the more popular branch of the controversy. I propose to notice only two or three of the arguments for the expediency of the protective tariff, and those I must take more by way of illustration.

During the recent political campaign the chief argument which was used was that the tariff made wages high. I have before me a circular which was widely distributed in which wage-receivers were told that free trade would either force employers to close their shops or to reduce their wages to foreign rates. In Germany the argument is that English workers get higher wages, which proves that they are better workmen, and that the Germans need protection against them. In America the argument is that the Englishmen do not get as good wages as the Americans, and that therefore the Americans need protection. The advantage of an empirical argument is that it goes as well one end foremost as the other. Suppose the Germans should argue like the Americans. They would then have to argue that free trade would *raise* their wages to the English rate, as the Americans argue that free trade would lower *their* wages to the English rate. Suppose the Americans should borrow the German argument. They would then have to argue that, as the Americans get higher wages, it proves that they are better workmen than the English, and need no protection against them, and *a fortiori* none against the workmen of the Continent.

There is one entirely American element in this argument, however. That is the claim or assumption that the high comfort of the American laborers is due to the tariff. One orator during the last campaign, who spoke with the authority of high official position, spoke with contempt and impatience of the low plane on which this tariff question is discussed, as if it were a mere question of dollars and cents, when in fact it is a question of status of the population and of the well-being of the wages classes.

We must distinguish here two propositions about wages which are constantly confused with each other, and which the protectionists find it very useful to confuse, altho they are inconsistent with each other, and both are false.

It is argued (1) that we want protection because wages are high, and (2) that we want protection in order to make wages high. To the legislature the high wages are represented as caused by some independent forces, and as a fact in the condition of the country which constitutes a reason for protection. To the workman it is argued that, the politicians and the employers having considered the matter and agreed that the American workingman ought to be well fed, clothed, etc., they have decided that he must have high wages, and that the tariff is the way to get them for him. This picture of the employers neglecting their business to lobby for a rise in the wages of their own men would be entertaining if it were not really so successful in deceiving those to whom it is addressed. The two branches of this argument about wages demand separate consideration.

1. Sociology is such a new science, and is as yet so little understood, that it is not strange if its doctrines have not yet spread very far through the community, but a superficial acquaintance with it would prevent any one from believing that politicians and statesmen can plan what sort of a people it would please them to have, or what degree of comfort they consider appropriate for the working classes. Nevertheless we have hundreds of politicians and orators who always start from a conception of this sort. It is evident, however, that the people of the United States must get their living out of the soil of the United States. We have an immense amount of land of the best quality, navigable rivers, great forests, mines of metal and coal, and we have to get out what we can with the labor and capital at our disposal. Whatever we get out will be distributed amongst us according to our shares in the production. As the natural stores are very rich and easy to get at, and as the laborers are few, it follows that the average product per laborer is greater than can be obtained in old countries, where the soil is more or less exhausted, and where the population is so dense as to make the competition of life very hard. This latter state of things affords us the second term of comparison by which we measure our status. Taken absolutely, there is plenty of room for improvement in our situation, and in the status of whole classes of our population.

We have, then, a perfectly obvious and sufficient explanation of the status of our people in natural facts. The statesmen have never planned this or done anything to help it. They have only marred it more or less. What we are is the result of our inherited traits and traditions, and of our physical surroundings. What there is about us which is good or bad, strong or weak, is alike to be attributed to these causes. High wages, therefore, or, more properly speaking, high average comfort, with little pauperism or misery, are incidents of our situation as early comers on a new continent. Yet there are people who tell us that they, in their wisdom, have made us well off by taxing us, and that we should not be so well off any more if we should get rid of the taxes, and they persuade the people who pay nearly all the taxes on consumption—namely, the artisans and laborers—that they could not get their living on this continent if they did not pay taxes. That is like telling a laborer who opens his dinner-pail that he would have more dinner if he would throw away a slice of bread.

This continent, however, is not so exclusively favored that it is likely to draw to itself all the population of the globe. Other continents have their advantages, and the one which has the best advantages for food and raw materials cannot in the nature of things have those advantages which come from a dense population and a high development of the arts and sciences. No one will be willing to turn away from the industries for which the country offers the best advantages to take up those in which other countries have the best advantages, unless the difference can be made up to him in some way. Hence manufacturing industry here has always had to contend with the profits possible in agricultural pursuits. Wages—so far as any wages class has ever yet been developed here—must be high enough to give the same scale of comfort as can be won in using land. The high wages and general high average of comfort are, therefore, plainly the same thing, and both proceed together out of the actual physical circumstances of the people.

What, then, can the tariff do about wages? It can only increase the wages in mechanical pursuits by deducting from the gains of agriculture. As we said above, it can win nothing for some without an equivalent or greater deduction from others. It no doubt draws upon each mechanical industry to make it help support all the others, and so it weakens them all; but whatever strength and help it brings to them as a group it must take from other groups. If, then, we are candidly seeking for the true effects of the restrictive system on the national welfare, and on the welfare of special classes, we must note that this operation cannot increase the national welfare, and we must look to see on whom it is that the corresponding loss falls. It is plain that it is upon the agricultural industries of the country, and accordingly a special bundle of fallacies has been devised for deceiving the agriculturists into the belief that they are gainers by it. It is evident, however, that every reduction in agricultural profits makes it easier for the employer to compete with the land for labor. The rising wages and the falling profits of agriculture meet each other at a point below what the profits of agriculture would be under freedom. If there were no tariff, the wages of the wages class must go up to the full measure of the agricultural profits under freedom. Hence the tariff lowers wages. It never has had and never can have any other effect. The employer in a protected industry pays no more than market rates for wages, and he could not possibly pay any less. The notion that he could lower wages to some foreign level in the midst of a country where labor could win higher rewards is of course absurd.

We see, then, that the argument that the tariff makes wages high is entirely without foundation. It has lowered wages. We see that the notion of having a tariff in order to secure to our people what they have as their birthright, and what the tariff only diminishes, viz., a comparatively better and easier existence than the people of older countries, is an imposture. It has very great popular effect because the popular notion is generally that we owe all our prosperity to ourselves and to what we call "our institutions," when in truth we owe everything that we are to historical antecedents and physical conditions.

Having stripped off this humbug from the issue, as stated by the protectionists, we may come back to the scornful complaint that we are discussing the question on a low level. We were told that we ought to debate it as a great question of status of the population, etc., and we have found that this was all rhetoric and fustian except the effect of the tariff to lower the status of the population. It follows, then, that we were right to debate it as a question of dollars and cents only. There is nothing else in it. A wants protection; that is, he wants B's money. B does not want to let him have it. A talks sentiment and metaphysics finely, and, after all, all there is in it is that he wants B's money. A does not otherwise show much interest in sentiment and patriotism and metaphysical goods generally. He never goes to Washington to lobby for education, or scientific research, or geographical exploration, or for any philanthropic scheme, unless there is a chance in it for him to get B's money. He is then moved to scorn at B's sordid love of money, and he goes to hear a lecture on "materialism" to gratify his wounded feelings because B will not give up his money. The matter is all stated from A's standpoint. We see him all the time. For him to want B's money is patriotic. It is "developing our resources." It is noble. For B to want to keep the same money is mean. I insist upon the matter being stated in the most crass and vulgar way, just because that is all there is of it when the humbug is all eliminated. The student of history then recognizes a very old friend. The robber-barons, Robin Hood, Dick Turpin, and others have had the same opinion of the nobility of wanting other people's money, and of the meanness of the "trader" or laborer who did not want to lose his earnings.

2. Let us next look at the other doctrine, that we need a protective tariff because wages are high; or the equivalent doctrine, that we cannot compete. The people of the United States can compete with anybody in getting wealth. The high wages are a proof of it; but they cannot compete with everybody else in every form of industry. They have only a limited number of laborers and a limited amount of capital. The same man cannot be doing two things at once. The same capital cannot be employed in two uses. Hence it will be wise and necessary to choose the *most* profitable of all the profitable employments which are possible. It will follow that we cannot afford to compete in any industry which will not pay here as well as those which have special advantages here. If we cannot compete, it is because we cannot afford to compete. We are too well off. We cannot compete with "foreign paupers," just because we are not paupers. "Pauper," of course, is one of those silly and invidious terms which have been introduced into this discussion in the interest of falsehood and folly. Paupers and

princes live in idleness supported by taxation. No one can compete with them. Seriously, then, we cannot compete with men who are fiercely competing with each other for low wages in a dense population because we are not fiercely competing with each other. We have abundant chances. The protectionists are not content, however, to use our advantages and avoid competition, which is what every sensible man does in private life. According to them we must go to seek competition. It will be told in history that a public bureau of our government spent part of the capital of the nation in seeking competition with Chinamen in making tea, at the very moment when the same government was trying to devise means to prevent Chinese competition in this country, where it could do no harm. As we shall seek competition with less favorably situated people only at a constant loss as compared with the gains we might win in our own favored industries, those who are carrying on the self-supporting industries must pay taxes to make up the loss, and the wealth of the country must undergo a constant waste. If a blacksmith should say that he could not compete with the shoemaker at making shoes, and therefore that he ought to be paid twice as much as the shoemaker for making shoes, his sanity would be doubted, but that is just the argument that we need a tariff because wages are high. It is because wages are high that we do not need one, and it is because we cannot compete in certain industries that we ought not to try. Some people think it is derogatory to us not to do everything for ourselves; and as they always seem glad to hear that we are exporting more and more, they seem to be desirous that we should make things for all the rest of the world too. What, then, I ask, is the rest of the world to do for us? If we take all the industries, how will they pay us for what we do for them? Competition is the force which under freedom indicates to us what we can do for ourselves and them, and what we can let them do for us to our final maximum advantage. To shut off competition and go into the industries which the ignorant empiricism of Congress or the caprice of individuals may select, is like unhinging the compass and steering the ship by chance.

3. There is no argument for the expediency of the tariff to be found in the matter of wages in any of its aspects, but it is

sometimes claimed that it is expedient to force certain industries into existence. This is called "developing our industries." We are good-natured enough to call them "our" industries, perhaps because we all pay taxes to support them, not because we own stock in them or participate in the profits. There is a very strong popular notion that it is a good thing for A, B, and C that there should be certain mills, factories, etc., up and down the country—a notion which has no support in fact at all, unless A, B, and C are owners of land near the factories, etc. If an individual were shown statistics of men employed, wages, capital, plant, output, etc., of a certain establishment, and were asked to invest in it, he would no doubt inquire, after all, whether the establishment made profits, since unfortunately not every big chimney does so; but when we are making speeches or writing essays about tariff, this last question is entirely ignored, and big figures and exclamation-points take the place of the only question which is important. If an industry does not pay, it is an industrial abomination. It is wasting and destroying. The larger it is the more mischief it does. The protected manufacturer is forced to allege, when he asks for protection, that his business would not pay without it. He proposes to waste capital. If he should waste his own wealth he would not go on long. He therefore asks the legislature to give him power to lay taxes on his fellow-citizens, to collect from them the capital which he intends to waste, and good wages for himself while he is carrying on that business besides. This is what is called "developing our industries," and the operation of the law is such that the waste and destruction can go on indefinitely. Either an industry can pay under freedom, in which case it does not need protection, or else it would not pay under freedom, in which case it is wasting the wealth of the nation as long as it goes on. It follows that the protective tariff is not a temporary expedient, and it is mathematically impossible that it should ever issue in an independent and productive industry. Other forces may come into play in time, viz., those which would at that time have called the industry in question into existence, and these forces may render the industry independent, but the tariff can never produce any such result.

4. Some have believed that the tariff system brought capital

into the country, and two or three instances of foreign manufacturers who have established branches here have been pointed to as triumphant proofs of it. I know of no statistics either of the amount of capital so imported or of the amount which the tariff has caused to be exported; but I should judge from such information as I have that one just about equalled the other. What is far more important, however, is that if the tariff were taken off any one of a great number of important articles, the people could save more capital in a month out of their diminished cost of living than all the capital which has been brought in here in twenty years on account of the tariff. A similar observation applies to the argument for deferring the reform of the tariff, that it would destroy capital now invested. No one proposes or desires any reckless action which would disregard vested interests of any kind, altho I do not see what difference it would make with what any one would really *do*, whether he had warning that the tariff would be repealed in five years or in five days; but that is a question for a statesman, and not for an economist. The economist may point out that, if any capital were destroyed, the savings of the people from a diminished cost of living would constitute an enormous fund for replacing that capital and offsetting that loss, so that, as far as the mere loss of capital is concerned, there would be no argument for delay.

5. I proceed to a brief but very cogent argument why a protective tariff is not expedient. Protection works all the time against improvement. In April, 1838, New York City indulged in great rejoicings over the arrival of the first steamships from Europe. In April, 1842, at an "Industrial Convention" held in New York City, the opening of steam navigation on the ocean was alleged as one of the chief arguments for protection. We are taxed to open our rivers and harbors, and the result is cheaper goods. That is the benefit which we anticipated and were working for, thinking that it would be a gain. As soon as it is realized, however, comes a clamor from home-producers of those kinds of goods which have been cheapened. "What! Do you mean to say that it is a good thing for the country to have people get the things which we make at a low price? This will never do;" and so a tax-barrier is set up across the rivers

and harbors to imitate the former barrier of sand and rock, and make things as dear and as hard to get as before. If protection is expedient, then this argument is sound, and we need more protection the more our communication with foreign nations is facilitated. Steamships, ocean cables, and cheap newspapers are all the time neutralizing the existing protection, and more taxes are necessary to give the same protection. If protection is sound, then those who rejoice over improvements in communication and transportation and support protection are guilty of absurd folly. If improvements, inventions, and discoveries are real benefits to mankind, then protection is inexpedient as well as philosophically absurd.

Commerce is plainly entering on a new stage. Common-sense makes its way very slowly into the minds of men when it has to rely on its own merits, but the course of progress in industry and commerce is such that self-interest often becomes hand-maid to common-sense, and then common-sense gets a chance. We have seen five or six new industries grow up in this country within a few years. They are all "land" industries; that is, they belong to the natural advantages of the country. They are in their infancy, but they are already great, and what they are to become no one can guess. They depend on a foreign market, and they have been made possible by cheap and quick ocean transit. Within a year a fleet of new steamers promises new growth in the same direction. The internal transportation of the country, especially in the West and South-west, will support the same growth. The effect is to cause great changes in the distribution of labor, great absorptions of capital in new orders of investments, and the creation of immense new interests. It would be overbold to predict specific results, but this much is clear: the competition of American agriculture will drive English labor and capital more exclusively into manufacturing and commerce. The complementary effect must be exerted here, and the profits of land industries will draw off labor and capital from manufactures and commerce. In other words, the international division of labor will be rendered more perfect, and the consequence must be greater wealth for all. But if the tariff still remains as a barrier to imports, *i.e.*, return cargoes, the exchanges must rule low to the detriment of all the exporting interests, and if specie is imported prices must advance. But the exports cannot rise, since they are forced to seek a foreign market. They will therefore be low, while everything else inside the country is high. This is, of course, the operation of the tariff now all the time, and it is the mode in which the tariff oppresses the land industries; but the whole course of the development which I am anticipating will be to make this oppression harder and sharper, while the tariff will all the time need to be raised higher and higher if it is to be of any avail at all. How long will the system stand such a double strain? If there is any industry which really depends upon the tariff, it cannot too soon begin to learn to do without it.